Raspberry Pi Robot with Camera and Sound using Python3.2
For Windows and Debian-Linux
Python runs on most operating systems

First Edition

Herb Norbom

Author of:
Raspberry Pi Camera Controls using Python 3.2.3
Raspberry Pi Camera Controls Python 2.7
Raspberry Pi Robot with Camera and Sound
Robot Wireless Control Made Simple with Python and C
Python Version 2.6 Introduction using IDLE
Python Version 2.7 Introduction using IDLE
Python Version 3.2 Introduction using IDLE and PythonWin
Bootloader Source Code for ATMega168 using STK500 For Microsoft Windows
Bootloader Source Code for ATMega168 using STK500 For Debian-Linux
Bootloader Source Code for ATMega328P using STK500 For Microsoft Windows
Bootloader Source Code for ATMega328P using STK500 For Debian-Linux
Books Available on Amazon and CreateSpace

Where we are aware of a trademark that name has been printed with a Capital Letter.

Great care has been taken to provide accurate information, by both the author and the publisher, no expressed or implied warranty of any kind is given. No liability is assumed for any damages in connection with any information provided.

Table of Contents

FOREWARD

The pace of improvement in the field of computers and science in general has been said to have become geometric. As you think of the technology that has become available to the average person and the advances reported you can probably sense that everything is accelerating. As computers become increasingly more powerful they will begin to blend with our bodies. While this may seem strange, I believe we will insist on it and pay through our noses for it. If you could not see, would you embrace technology that gave you sight? If you could not walk, would you be willing to have a computer give you the ability? I think many people would. As computers race to the day of singularity the question may well become will they be our closest relative or our worst enemy? Given the pace of change we have less time to think about this than you might imagine.

PREFACE

This is a continuation story for the evolution of MAX the robot introduced in my first book. No you will not have to buy the first book to use this one. In the first book MAX used the ATmega328P chip with an H-Bridge for the two wheel drive. The eye, if you will, was a Foscam Fi8910W Camera. The communication to the robot was with a serial port device converter and a Wireless Transceiver. On the PC, Python 2.7 was used to build a control platform. The Atmega328P used a C program for its on-board control. MAX could play wav files and had Text to Speech capabilities. MAX also had a wooden arm that was moved by a servo. The camera consumed a lot of power and overall the communications were not great for the camera or the Wireless Transceiver. Anyone who has worked with serial ports will probably have stories of how irrational and erratic the port is.

While MAX worked I knew that an upgrade would be needed. What I wanted to accomplish with an upgrade can be summarized as follows:

- Increase communication reliability
- Decrease power requirements
- Increase on-board capabilities – memory, control pins, processing speed, etc
- Get to one programming language
- Ability to operate from a Debian-Linux or Windows control platform
- Keep or expand existing capabilities

As I looked around at the possibilities I became intrigued with the Raspberry Pi. Needing to stay out of my wife's hair, I ordered the Raspberry Pi. While I used the Raspberry Pi off and on, I was not quite convinced that it was the way I wanted to go. Then the Raspberry Pi came out with a camera and after getting that working I was sold. I made the upgrade using Python 2.7 as shown in the book "Raspberry Pi Robot with Camera and Sound". The latest release of the wheezy operating system includes Python 3.2.3 and 'tkinter'. I also wanted to add information on the battery for powering the Raspberry Pi. My future enhancements will be using Python 3.2.3 or latter. For these reasons I wanted to update the book. Once again you do not need to purchase previous versions of the book as this book will include all that information.

As a point of reference I am currently running Microsoft Windows XP Professional Version 2002 Service Pack 3 on a Dell Dimension PC with Pentium4 CPU 3.00GHz. I am also running Debian Release 6.0.7 (squeeze) on an old PC with an Intel(R) Pentium(R) 4 CPU 2.40GHz. The Kernel Linux is 2.6.32-5-686. I am also using the GNOME Desktop 2.30.2 using the bash shell. The Raspberry Pi is running Linux Raspbian, Kernel 3.6.11, version wheezy, built from 2013-09-25-wheezy-raspbian.zip, and the Debian-Linux version is 7.2. We will use the installed Python 3.2.3 software. My home network utilizes a Netgear router.

So to get started I have listed the steps we will go through. As far as setting up the Raspberry Pi I am not going to go very far into that, but I do provide a summary in the Appendix. There are excellent sources on line, no use building a new wheel. But get the biggest SD card you can. The 4GB just will work, but bigger is better. At this point my Pi disk is consuming less than 2GB.

While we are going to setup the Raspberry Pi to be operational without a monitor, keyboard or mouse I suggest that as you are learning and testing that you leave those items connected.

Why Python?

Even If you have never programmed before, I suggest you start with Python. We are going to be using a lot of Python. While I am sure everyone has their own favorite programming language and good reasons for it, at this point Python is my choice. As you learn Python you will gain insight into areas you are going to need to control your robot. There are several reasons for choosing Python, they include the following:
- Object Oriented – will flow with events rather than straight lines
- Not compiled, uses an interpreter – therefore, quick results while developing applications
- Runs on Windows, Linux, Unix, even Apple – it is portable
- There is lot of FREE information on the web about it
- Python is free and already installed on your Raspberry Pi
- There are a lot of free modules - you may need to enhance your project
- What you learn, program flow and structure will to some extent carry over to C, C++ or C#, or whatever language you evolve to
- Python has a good built-in GUI, tkinter

Yes, of course there are disadvantages, if you are going to do something for resale Python may not be the language for you. If you are here, you are probably not close to having anything to sell, so don't worry about that. Just because Python uses an interpreter do not think you are limited in terms of program size and complexity. The Raspberry Pi has multiple versions of Python installed. As of this time Python 2.7.3 is the default version. We are going to use Python 3.2.3 which is also installed. We are going to write our programs on the Raspberry Pi and when finished we will be able to operate our robot from either a Windows PC or a Debian-Linux PC. If you are not familiar with Python at all consider the book 'Python Version 3.2 Introduction using IDLE and PythonWin' sold on Amazon, yes I am the author, sorry about the self promoting. While I am going to provide the complete source code I am not going to go into the same depth in explaining the code as I did in my first book 'Robot Wireless Control Made Simple with Python and C'. If you are interested you can search Amazon using my name for a complete list of books.

PROCESS STEPS

- Of course you need the Raspberry Pi and various hardware items listed under Supplies and Devices. You will need to get the Pi working over a wireless communication.

- You are going to be downloading software, if you do not have a high speed connection this is going to be very difficult.

- You need to setup your directories, just makes life easier.

- We will write our Programs using Python 3.2.3 as that is installed on the Raspberry Pi and it is an excellent choice anyway. Also 'tkinter' is installed with this version of Python.

- We are going to build a robot. The robot described in the book uses two wheel drive. In the Appendix I have listed the parts I used. What your robot looks like is entirely up to you.

Supplies and Devices

The following parts list can be viewed as a starting point, substitute as you like. A parts list for the robot is included in the Appendix. The Raspberry Pi is sold by a number of distributors. Prices shown are what I paid and they will probably have changed.

Part	Possible Source	Source Part #	Min Qty	Approx. Price	Ext. Price
Raspberry Pi Model B 512MB	AdaFruit	ID: 998	1	39.95	39.95
Linear Regulator-5V	Mouser Electronics	511-L7805CV	2	0.59	1.18
5V Micro USB AC Adapter	MCM	28-13060	1	6.61	6.61
Wireless N NANO USB Adapter 802.11b	MCM	831-2761	1	14.99	14.99
Resistor Kit –for selection	Electronix Express	13RK7305	1	11.95	11.95
Capacitor Kit -for selection	Elecronix Express	32DLXCAPKIT	1	14.95	14.95
Half-Size Bread Board	AdaFruit	ID:64	1	5.00	5.00
Tiny Breadboard (get 2)	AdaFruit	ID:65	2	4.00	8.00
Hook Up Wire 22AWG solid core	get best price	you do not need a lot for this project			
Raspberry Pi Camera Board	AdaFruit	ID: 805	1	29.95	29.95
LED find a good source get a bag of them(get various colors)	AllElectronics (buy several)	CAT #LED-1 there are many to choose from	5	0.07	0.35
Desktop High Speed USB2.0 Hub with Power Supply	Find best one. Need while testing.	Check for one working with Raspberry	1		
SD Memory Card(min4GB)	AdaFruit	many choices available	1		
SD Memory Card Reader/Writer	Find best one	very possible your computer has one	1		
Prototying Pi Plate Kit for Raspberry Pi	AdaFruit	ID: 801 Optional but is a nice addition	1	15.95	15.95

Part	Possible Source	Source Part #	Min Qty	Approx. Price	Ext. Price
H-Bridge there are various suppliers of them – get one with diodes	Mouser or wherever but get the Data sheet	595-SN75441ONE	1	2.34	2.34

I did not include a monitor, keyboard or mouse, hopefully you have spares to use while you get everything running; it is possible to run the Pi without them. We will not need them once all is working and that includes the USB Hub. For resistors this project requires only a couple but I suggest the kit so you have size selection. The same for the capacitor, I am using only one 35V capacitor. If you are buying from Electronix Express consider the capacitor kits, as there is a minimum order limit of $20.00. For the breadboard, I will be using the Tiny Breadboard, but any will work. A good idea is to buy several breadboards of different sizes. On your order of LED's get a bunch, price is low and you should expect to burn some up. For all of the items listed this is a possible parts and POSSIBLE supplier list. For the low priced items you may want to buy several as multiple shipments will end up costing more. For the Raspberry items in particular check out the package deals that are available. While I have used these suppliers I am not saying they are the best or the least expensive. I am not affiliated with any of them.

While I did not put batteries on the preceding list you are going to need some. Take a look at the section on Raspberry Pi power.

Work Directories-Raspberry Pi

We are going to be writing a number of programs and it can get very confusing where they are located. Also from a backup view point it is nice to have them in a separate directory, probably several. I suggest you make a separate directory now. I called my directory 'MAX3' in the Pi home directory.

Setup Windows PC

For our remote control we are going to need some software on the PC. There are a number of options but I am just going to list what I was able to get working. You are going to need PuTTY and Xming. PuTTY provides the communication link and Xming provides the X11 capabilities for our PC. What we are going to do is have our Raspberry Pi running and then from our Windows PC log on to the Raspberry as 'root'. Now I know you are probably saying no I will not. I will use 'pi' or another user account. That will work to some extent. The reason I am having you log-in as root is that I have not been able to access GPIO <u>AND</u> run Python tkinter unless I use root. To access GPIO you need to use root or sudo. To have tkinter work you need to either log-in as root or as just a regular user. If you use sudo you will lose tkinter. I tried a number of variations and decided that my Raspberry Pi is just being used by me and logging in as root was just plain easier. I am not worried about other users messing thinks up. After all I can do that, and have many times. So beware, we will be accessing the Raspberry Pi from our Windows or Debian-Linux PC using SSH connection over a wireless network and logging in as root. The change to access GPIO as a regular user may have been made by the time you read this, you may want to try as a regular user first. As I recall root had to be setup on my Raspberry Pi, see the Appendix for that information.

See the Appendix for downloading PuTTY and for setup. Xming is also covered in the Appendix. With everything working we will log on to the Raspberry Pi using 'root'.

Setup Debian-Linux PC

If you are going to run your robot from Debian-Linux you will need to add software to the Raspberry Pi as well as to your Debian-Linux PC. While just logging in to the Pi is easy, running a GUI is a little more difficult.   From a Terminal prompt on the Debian-Linux PC enter the following command:

$ ssh -X 192.168.1.9 -l root   You will need to have enabled ssh on the Pi.(See Appendix for information)

Change the IP address to match where your Pi is connected. Note the capital X and the small letter L in front of root. See the Appendix for an illustration.

Whether you are using Debian-Linux or Windows you can run your Pi 'headless' (without a monitor). It is easier to set everything up with the Pi having a monitor, keyboard and mouse. In the Appendix I provide information and illustrations for the setup process.

Program or Text Editor

I am going to install Geany on my Raspberry Pi, on my Windows PC and on the Debian-Linux PC, see the Appendix for installation information. You can use any text editor you like, that includes Python's Idle, nano, vi or vim or whatever you like. Each has pluses and minuses.   A very nice feature of Geany is that you can run the program right from Geany. Once you are running the program remotely or as they say 'headless' with no monitor attached you may appreciate this feature.

Python Start

The Raspberry Pi may need to have additional libraries installed for working with GPIO. The latest version of wheezy has the library installed. (See Appendix) The following walks you through your first Python program using a Windows PC. The process for running from Debian-Linux is similar to the Windows process. See the Appendix for getting this working. Once you are logged onto the Pi from either the Windows PC or the Debian-Linux PC the process becomes the same because you are running from the Pi.

First let us make a very small Python program. I have installed Geany on the Raspberry Pi and I have logged onto the Raspberry Pi from my Windows PC using PuTTY, log-in as root. I have Xming running on the PC at this point.   I suggest you change to our MAX3 directory. Enter from the # prompt:

'cd /home/pi/MAX3'.

Before we write our first program script I suggest you type 'python3' at the # prompt as shown in Illustration1.

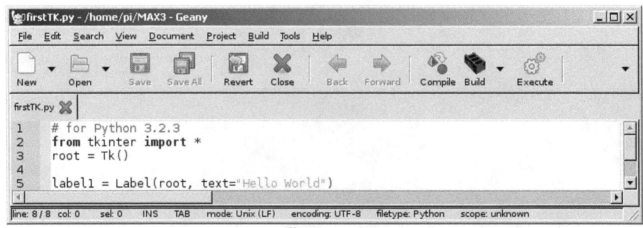

Illustration 1

If you get the Python prompt you can enter "Crtl z" to exit Python and return to the # prompt.

With Python working let us write our first script using Geany. (You will need to have Xming working, see Appendix for that installation.) Enter 'geany' at the # prompt. Go ahead and enter the program code and save file as 'firstTK.py'. The 'py' extension is required by Python and Geany also uses it to identify the script type.

```python
# for Python 3.2.3
from tkinter import *
root = Tk()

label1 = Label(root, text="Hello World")
```

Illustration 2

One of the many nice things about Geany is that you can execute the script without leaving Geany. First let us make sure that the execute command in Geany is correct. Click on 'Build' and select 'Set Build Commands'. Under the last items on the screen you should see Execute as python "%f". That is the only command we are interested in at this point. (The "%f" is your program name that Geany enters automatically for you.) Note that it is calling Python and not Python3. You have choices you can change the command to python3"%f" or add a command, or as I have done add a new command to just be python and change the existing command to python3.

Set Build Commands

#	Label	Command	Working directory	Reset
Python commands				
1.	Compile	python -m py_compile "%f"		🔒
2.				🔒
3.				🔒
Error regular expression:				🔒
Independent commands				
1.	Make	make		🔒
2.	Make Custom Target	make		🔒
3.	Make Object	make %e.o		🔒
4.				🔒
Error regular expression:				🔒

Note: Item 2 opens a dialogue and appends the response to the command.

Execute commands				
1.	Execute	python3 "%f"		🔒
2.	EXprompt	python "%f"		🔒

%d, %e, %f, %p are substituted in command and directory fields, see manual for details.

Cancel   OK

Illustration 3

Click OK or Cancel to close the window. To run the Python script, click on the Execute button. A LXTerminal window will open and our tkinter window will be open on it. If you want to run python 2.7 scripts select EXprompt from the Build Menu.

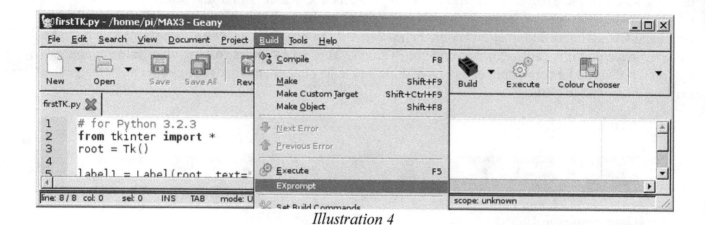

Illustration 4

Illustration 5

Our tkinter window also shows.

This works like a normal window, click on the x to close. When you close the tkinter window the LXTerminal window will prompt you with the message "Press return to continue", the LXTerminal closes when you press return.

If you had problems with this you may want to try running directly from your Raspberry Pi console. We need to have this working before proceeding. If you can, take some time and explore the features of Geany. If you want to run Geany from the console you need to have Xwindows running. If you are running from Gnome or LXDE you may see Geany on the menu. If not there select LXTerminal or root terminal and run from that window by typing 'geany'.

I am sure you are aware, but just in case I need to mention how to shutdown your Pi. You should always run a 'shutdown' procedure. These procedures ensure an orderly closing of files and help prevent corruption of your SD. A good procedure is "shutdown -h now", if not logged in as root you need to precede the command with "sudo".

PYTHON and GPIO

You are going to need the General Purpose Input/Output library called the GPIO library, see the Appendix. With this latest version of wheezy the library has been installed for you. As you are aware the Raspberry Pi uses the Broadcom BCM2835 system.   This provides from our perspective the naming conventions of the GPIO pins. You need to do a little research to be certain which Raspberry Pi version you have. At this point the latest version is REV 2 for the GPIO pins. This information will be based on REV2. I added the Adafruit Pi Proto Plate/801 to my Raspberry Pi. If you go this route you do need to do some soldering. You will be better off getting some kind of interface plate to work with. It is very easy to 'brick' or 'fry' your Pi and these plates make it a little safer.   One of the more confusing items of GPIO is that the GPIO names do not match the PIN numbers. To make matters worse there are two ways of numbering the IO pins on the Raspberry Pi within RPi.GPIO. The method we are going to use is the BOARD numbering system. With this method we will refer to the pin numbers on the P1 header of the Raspberry Pi. With this method our hardware should always work regardless of the board revision of the RPi.   The second numbering system is for BCM numbers, or the Broadcom numbering system. One of the reasons I prepared the following is to help visualize the P1 relation to the Proto Plate. To add just a little more confusion the Proto Plate that I have uses the BCM numbering system.

	GPIO	This is Layout for the Ptroto Plate Rev2 Pin as shown below	A good reference
With the Adafruit Pi Proto Plate/801 mounted on the RaspberryPi

A good reference
http://elinux.org/RPi_Low-level_peripherals
IF YOU USE BCM GPIO the GPIO will
match the Pin # when we select in Python

	GPIO	Rev2 Pin	
3.3V		1	
GND		6	
GND		6	
5V		2	
MOSI	GPIO 10	19	
MISO	GPIO 9	21	
SLCK	GPIO 11	23	
CS0	GPIO 8	24	Not sure here board says CS0, but I think it might be CE0
CS1	GPIO 7	26	Not sure here board says CS1, but I think it might be CE1

Proto Plate Coding	SDA	SCL	TXD	RXD	#17	#18	21/27	#22	#23	#24	#25	#4	5V	GND	3V3	GND
Rev2 Pin	3		8	10	11	12		15	16	18	22	7	2	6	1	9
GPIO REF	2	3	14	15	17	12		22	23	24	25	4				

Note I do not know which GND pin where there are several
Note I do not know which 5V or 3v pin where there are several

To get a feel for how RaspberryPI pins are setup consider the 26 pin Expansion Header (P1 on the Raspberry)

Expansion Header or GPIO Connector(P1)

the old Layout	Bottom Row		Top Row	
REV1 Layout		REV 2 LAYOUT		Maximum permitted current draw
	3V3 Power	P1 2	5V POWER	from 3.3 V pins	50mA
GPIO 0	GPIO 2 (I2C0 SDA)	3 4	5V POWER	from 5 V pins	1A
GPIO 1	GPIO 3 (I2C0 SLC)	5 6	GROUND	
	GPIO 4 (GPCLK0)	7 8	GPIO 14 (TXD UART0_TXD)	
	GROUND	9 10	GPIO 15 (RXD UART0_RXD)	
	GPIO 17	11 12	GPIO 18 (PCM_CLK)	
GPIO 21	GPIO 27 (PCM_DIN)	13 14	GROUND	
	GPIO 22	15 16	GPIO 23	
	3V3 Power	17 18	GPIO 24	
	GPIO 10(SPIO MOSI)	19 20	GROUND	
	GPIO 9 (SPIO MISO)	21 22	GPIO 25	
	GPIO 11 (SPIO SLCK)	23 24	GPIO 8 (SPIO CEO)	
	GROUND	25 26	GPIO 7 (SPIO CE1)	

P5 Header (Located next to SD card reader)   **Look at from bottom of RaspberryPI card**
production model does not have connector pins, just the perf socket

5V	P1 2	3V3
GPIO28	3 4	GPIO29
GPIO30	5 6	GPIO31
GND	7 8	GND

P6 Header (located near HDMI input)
production model does not have connector pins, just the perf socket
Reset button ADD , short the two pins for soft reset

Illustration 6

Double check the labeling, there could be revisions, it is convoluted and possible errors may have crept in.

Python Test PWM with LED

This will be a short Python program to test PWM and get you a little familiar with the GPIO process and how we will wire the board. Let us get the program running first then we can wire the breadboard. Anytime you are working with the Raspberry Pi and/or the Proto Board be careful. Hooking something up incorrectly can fry your board. Double check all connections and prove what I suggest rather than just using blind faith. I will not be responsible for any damages. The Raspberry Pi GPIO pins are unprotected. Do remember that static electricity is not your friend, ground yourself prior to working with components. In the following illustration you may note that I turned off the tool bars, yes it is still Geany. You will continue to need to log-in as 'root' anytime we are accessing GPIO and using tkinter.

The program asks for your input, you can use lower or upper case, the program converts it to upper case. The program also asks for a speed or power in the form of a single digit integer.

You can run the program and get the bugs out before we do our wiring. If you want to run from the console make sure you are logged in as root. You will need to select 'xterm' for it to run correctly. Start the GUI (from the # prompt type startx) then select LXTerminal or xterm from the menu.

If you are having problems getting the LED to light, test it. I know I have lost time debugging something that worked. Remember which way your LED works. The long wire is for + (Anode) and the shorter leg or wire for – (Cathode). The short leg goes to ground. The resistor is to limit current so the LED doesn't blow up or burn out to quickly. There are web sites to help you with calculations.

As we will begin using the GPIO module now it is somewhat important for you to exit the program using the exit routines. While you can just close the window that does not clean up the GPIO pin settings.

File   Edit   Search   View   Document   Project   Build   Tools   Help

testingPWMBOARD.py ✖

```
 1     #Python 3.2.3
 2     import sys
 3     from time import sleep
 4     import RPi.GPIO as GPIO
 5     GPIO.setmode(GPIO.BOARD)           #use Raspberri Pi pin coding BOARD
 6     GPIO.setup(15, GPIO.OUT)           #On Proto Board shows as GPIO22
 7     GPIO.setup(16, GPIO.OUT)           #On Proto Board shows as GPIO23
 8     gpioversionBCM=GPIO.BCM                 #for Information only not using
 9     print ('GPIO VersionBCM: ' ,gpioversionBCM)
10     gpioversion=GPIO.BOARD                       #for Information only
11     print ('GPIO Version: ' ,gpioversion)
12     gpioRevision =GPIO.RPI_REVISION              #for Information only
13     print ('GPIO Revision: ', gpioRevision)
14     gpioversion2=GPIO.VERSION                    #for Information only
15     print ('GPIO Version2: ' ,gpioversion2)
16
17     def pin15():         #Select 'L'    On Proto Board shows as GPIO22
18         p1 = GPIO.PWM(15, 50)         # Channel, Frequency
19         p1.start(0)
20         try:
21             for power in range (0,100,5):
22                 p1.ChangeDutyCycle(power)
23                 print (power)
24                 sleep(0.1)
25             for power in range(100, 0, -5):
26                 p1.ChangeDutyCycle(power)
27                 print (power)
28                 sleep(0.1)
29         except:
30             pass
31         p1.ChangeDutyCycle(0)        #turn off power
32         p1.stop()
```

This is Geany 1.22.

Illustration 7

File Edit Search View Document Project Build Tools Help

testingPWMBOARD.py ✖

```python
33  def pin16(speed):      #Select 'R'        On Proto Board shows as GPIO23
34      p2 = GPIO.PWM(16, 50)        # Channel, Frequency
35      p2.start(speed)
36      sleep(2.1)
37      p2.ChangeDutyCycle(0)        #turn off power
38      p2.stop()
39  def stop():           # Select 'X'
40      GPIO.output(15, False)   #False sets output to LOW,
41      GPIO.output(16, 0)       #False is also a 0
42      print ('program stop ordered')
43      GPIO.cleanup()           # resets all pins used by this program
44      sys.exit(0)
45  while True:
46      cmd = input("Command, L/R 0..9, X=stop  E.g. L5 :")
47      try:
48          direction = cmd[0].upper()  # convert contents to uppercase
49      except:
50          stop()
51      print (direction)
52      if direction !="X":
53          try:
54              speed = int(cmd[1]) * 11
55          except:
56              speed = 0
57      else:
58          speed = 0
59      print (speed)
60      if direction == "L":
61          pin15()
62      elif direction == "R":
63          pin16(speed)
64      elif direction =="X":
65          stop()
66      else:
67          stop()
68
```

line: 68 / 68   col: 0   sel: 0   INS   TAB   mode: Unix (LF)   encoding: UTF-8   filetype: Python   scope: stop

Illustration 8

Raspberry Pi Robot with Camera and Sound using Python 3.2   Page 15

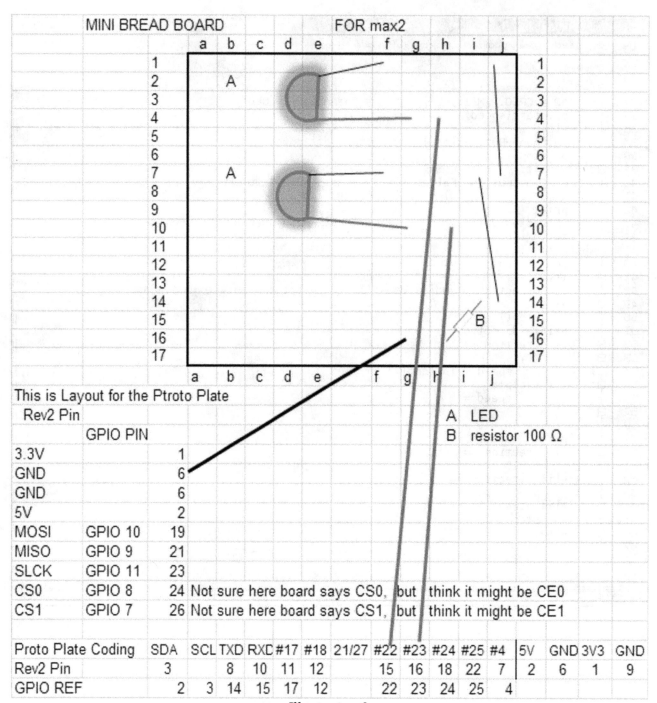

MINI BREAD BOARD   FOR max2

This is Layout for the Ptroto Plate

Rev2 Pin					A	LED
	GPIO PIN				B	resistor 100 Ω
3.3V		1				
GND		6				
GND		6				
5V		2				
MOSI	GPIO 10	19				
MISO	GPIO 9	21				
SLCK	GPIO 11	23				
CS0	GPIO 8	24	Not sure here board says CS0, but I think it might be CE0			
CS1	GPIO 7	26	Not sure here board says CS1, but I think it might be CE1			

Proto Plate Coding	SDA	SCL	TXD	RXC	#17	#18	21/27	#22	#23	#24	#25	#4	5V	GND	3V3	GND
Rev2 Pin	3		8	10	11	12		15	16	18	22	7	2	6	1	9
GPIO REF		2	3	14	15	17	12		22	23	24	25	4			

Illustration 9

Illustration 10

One more test program to introduce PWM; still using LED, but with tkinter. We will use the same board, but work with only the one LED. In this test we want to vary the intensity of the LED and the frequency, or rate of off/on. After you have it working, watch the LED as you enter different values for Power and Frequency.

File   Edit   Search   View   Document   Project   Build   Tools   Help

testingGPIO_BOARDtkinter.py ✖

```python
1    #python 3.2.3
2    import sys
3    from time import sleep
4    from tkinter import *
5    import RPi.GPIO as GPIO
6    GPIO.setmode(GPIO.BOARD)            #use Raspberri Pi pin Rev2 coding
7
8    def Test():
9        global p15, p15freq
10       print ('Light Test Power= ',p15power,' Freq= ', p15freq)
11       p15=GPIO.PWM(15, p15freq) # Channel, Frequency(lenght of pulse)
12       p15.start(0)   #need to start the or pulse
13       try:
14           p15.ChangeDutyCycle(p15power)
15           sleep(0.3)
16       except:
17           pass
18       p15.ChangeDutyCycle(0)         # don't forget this to turn off
19
20   def incPower():
21       global p15power
22       p15power=p15power +10
23       if p15power > 99:
24           p15power=100
25
26   def decPower():
27       global p15power
28       p15power=p15power -10
29       if p15power < 1:
30           p15power=0
31   def incFreq():
32       global p15freq
33       p15freq=p15freq +10
34       if p15freq > 99:
35           p15freq=100
36   def decFreq():
37       global p15freq
38       p15freq=p15freq -10
39       if p15freq <1:
40           p15freq=.1
```

line: 76 / 81   col: 40   sel: 0   INS   TAB   mode: Unix (LF)   encoding: UTF-8   filetype: Python   scope: YouStop

Illustration 11

File   Edit   Search   View   Document   Project   Build   Tools   Help

testingGPIO_BOARDtkinter.py ✖

```
41  def YouStop():
42      global p15
43      print ( 'program stop ordered' )
44      GPIO.cleanup()
45      top.quit()
46      sys.exit(0)
47
48  if __name__=='__main__':
49      top = Tk()
50      top.title("Control Light " )
51      Button(top, text="Click to Light", command=Test,
52          bg='gold').grid(column=0, row=1, sticky=(N,W,S))
53      label = Label(top, text='Hello from Tkinter land')
54      label.grid(column=0, row=2, sticky=(N,W,S))
55      stop = Button(top, text='QUIT', command=YouStop,
56          bg='red', fg='white')
57      stop.grid(column=0, row=3, sticky=(N,W,S))
58      PowerIncp15 = Button(top, text='INC Power', command=incPower,
59          bg='brown', fg='white')
60      PowerIncp15.grid(column=0, row=4, sticky=(N,W,S))
61      PowerDecp15 = Button(top, text='DEC Power', command=decPower,
62          bg='green', fg='white')
63      PowerDecp15.grid(column=0, row=5, sticky=(N,W,S))
64      Freqinc15 = Button(top, text='INC Frequency', command=incFreq,
65          bg='red', fg='white')
66      Freqinc15.grid(column=0, row=6, sticky=(N,W,S))
67      Freqdec15 = Button(top, text='Decrease Frequency', command=decFreq,
68          bg='red', fg='white')
69      Freqdec15.grid(column=0, row=7, sticky=(N,W,S))
70
71      print ('PIN15 or GPIO15 shown as GPIO22 on PROTO PLATE')
72      print ('SETUP THE PIN as OUTPUT')
73      GPIO.setup(15, GPIO.OUT)
74      print ('#test to read GPIO')
75      print (' if 0 then pin is high as getting False, so is output')
76      print ('GPIO22 is: ',GPIO.input(15))
77      global p15, p15power, p15freq
78      p15freq = 50
79      p15power=75
80      mainloop()
81
```

line: 81 / 81   col: 0   sel: 0   INS   TAB   mode: Unix (LF)   encoding: UTF-8   filetype: Python   scope: YouStop

Illustration 12

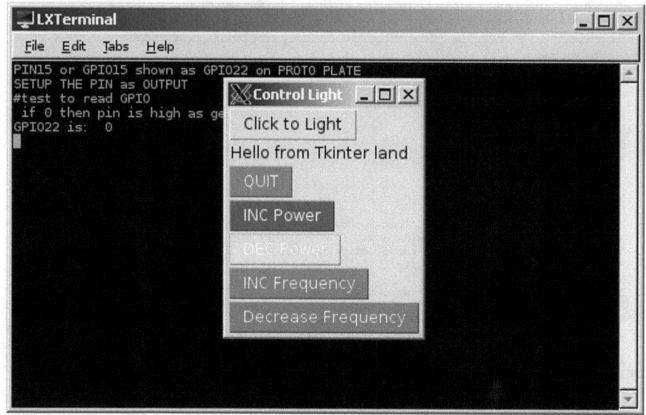

Illustration 13

Wire H-Bridge

For our next step I want to get our H-Bridge working. The H-Bridge test program will use tkinter for control. As we will be working with GPIO, you must log in as root. Go ahead and get your program running prior to hooking up to the breadboard. Once you are ready double check the connections and the instructions provided. At this point we will be adding relatively low power to the H-Bridge as external power. Be aware that as you progress you will add higher auxiliary power. If you plug into a GPIO pin in error you will fry the Raspberry Pi GPIO pins. No need to prove it, I did by accident.

```
1    #Python 3.2.3  Herb RyMax, Inc. 11/13/2013
2    import sys
3    from time import sleep
4    from tkinter import *
5    import RPi.GPIO as GPIO
6    GPIO.setmode(GPIO.BOARD)        #use Raspberri Pi pin Rev2 coding
7    def fwd():
8        print ('at fwd')
9        GPIO.setup(16, GPIO.IN)        #turn off
10       GPIO.setup(22, GPIO.IN)
11       GPIO.setup(15, GPIO.OUT)       # SETUP THE PIN as OUTPUT'
12       GPIO.setup(18, GPIO.OUT)
13       p15=GPIO.PWM(15, 50) # Channel, Frequency(lenght of pulse)
14       p18=GPIO.PWM(18, 50)
15       try:
16           p15.start(p15power)
17           p18.start(p18power)
18           sleep(1.3)
19       except:
20           pass
21       GPIO.setup(15, GPIO.IN)
22       GPIO.setup(18, GPIO.IN)
23   def rev():
24       print ('at rev')
25       GPIO.setup(15, GPIO.IN)        #turn off
26       GPIO.setup(18, GPIO.IN)
27       GPIO.setup(16, GPIO.OUT)       # SETUP THE PIN as OUTPUT'
28       GPIO.setup(22, GPIO.OUT)
29       p16=GPIO.PWM(16, 50) # Channel, Frequency(lenght of pulse)
30       p22=GPIO.PWM(22, 50)
31       try:
32           p16.start(p16power)
33           p22.start(p22power)
34           sleep(1.3)
35       except:
36           pass
37       GPIO.setup(16, GPIO.IN)
38       GPIO.setup(22, GPIO.IN)
```

line: 43 / 63   col: 0   sel: 0   INS   TAB   mode: Unix (LF)   encoding: UTF-8   filetype: Python   scope: YouStop

Illustration 14

Raspberry Pi Robot with Camera and Sound using Python 3.2   Page 21

File   Edit   Search   View   Document   Project   Build   Tools   Help

GPIO_BOARDtkinterH_Bridge.py ✖

```
39
40   def YouStop():
41       print ('program stop ordered')
42       GPIO.cleanup()
43       root.quit()
44       sys.exit(0)
45
46   if __name__=='__main__':
47       root = Tk()
48       root.title("Control Light " )
49       Button(root, text="Click Forward", command=fwd,
50           bg='green').grid(column=0, row=1, sticky=(N,W,S))
51       Button(root, text="Click Reverse", command=rev,
52           bg='red').grid(column=0, row=2, sticky=(N,W,S))
53       stop = Button(root, text='QUIT', command=YouStop,
54           bg='black', fg='white')
55       stop.grid(column=0, row=3, sticky=(N,W,S))
56       global p15power, p18power
57       global p16power, p22power
58       p15power=50      #you may want to adjust depending on what
59       p18power=50      #you are hooking up, try 75 for a LED
60       p16power=50      #try 50 for a small motor
61       p22power=50
62       mainloop()
63
```

line: 63 / 63   col: 0   sel: 0   INS   TAB   mode: Unix (LF)   encoding: UTF-8   filetype: Python   scope: YouStop

Illustration 15

For our first pass I am using four LED's and a TI H-Bridge. To keep the voltage low I am powering the H-Bridge with the 5V supply from the Raspberry Pi. To power the TI Auxiliary Power I am using the Raspberry Pi 3.3V supply and running it through a 33 ohm resistor. I have prepared the following illustration to assist you in wiring your breadboard.

BREAD BOARD Testing H-Bridge using LED's

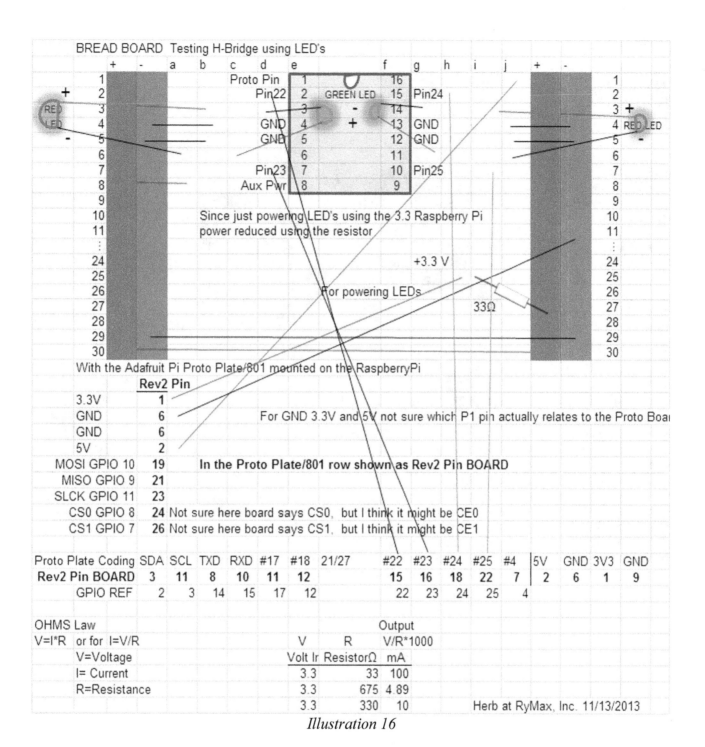

Since just powering LED's using the 3.3 Raspberry Pi power reduced using the resistor

+3.3 V

For powering LEDs

33Ω

With the Adafruit Pi Proto Plate/801 mounted on the RaspberryPi

	Rev2 Pin	
3.3V	1	
GND	6	
GND	6	For GND 3.3V and 5V not sure which P1 pin actually relates to the Proto Boar
5V	2	
MOSI GPIO 10	19	**In the Proto Plate/801 row shown as Rev2 Pin BOARD**
MISO GPIO 9	21	
SLCK GPIO 11	23	
CS0 GPIO 8	24	Not sure here board says CS0, but I think it might be CE0
CS1 GPIO 7	26	Not sure here board says CS1, but I think it might be CE1

Proto Plate Coding	SDA	SCL	TXD	RXD	#17	#18	21/27	#22	#23	#24	#25	#4	5V	GND	3V3	GND
Rev2 Pin BOARD	3	11	8	10	11	12		15	16	18	22	7	2	6	1	9
GPIO REF	2	3	14	15	17	12		22	23	24	25	4				

OHMS Law

V=I*R   or for I=V/R

V=Voltage

I= Current

R=Resistance

	Output	
V	R	V/R*1000
Volt Ir	ResistorΩ	mA
3.3	33	100
3.3	675	4.89
3.3	330	10

Herb at RyMax, Inc. 11/13/2013

Illustration 16

Illustration 17

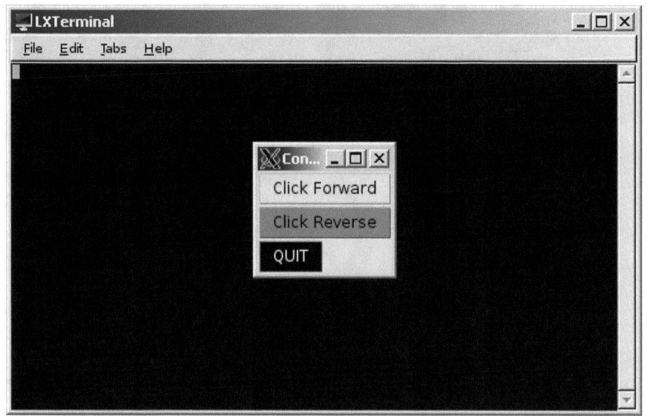

Illustration 18

H-BRIDGE WITH SMALL MOTOR

Now that you have the H-Bridge running it is time to try some small motors. We will use the same program, "GPIO_BOARDtkinterH_Bridge.py" to run our tests. For our first test I took out both of the LED's on the left side. I left in the right side so a light would show in case the motor did not turn. I am using a small motor from a toy fan; you should get a short spin from the motor. Other than planning the spin direction of the motor it doesn't matter which motor connections you use on the H-Bridge. You can connect the positive motor terminal to either H-Bridge pin 2 or pin 7. Just connect the negative motor terminal to the other H-Bridge pin. If you have problems it is possible that your motor draws more power than we are providing. You can try eliminating the resistor and or providing 5V power. Think any change through. If it works leave it for now as we will be working on more power for the motors shortly.

Illustration 19

ROBOT CONTROL PROGRAMS

I think we have covered the basics and we should now be able to design our actual control panel. While we are testing I am going to leave the Raspberry Pi and the breadboard setup just as we had from our previous test. In our new program I want to 'fancy' up the code a bit. We are going to define classes and eliminate most of the global variables. We are also going to build our program in modules. In the long run modules will make life easier, maybe not so much in the short run. As there is a fair amount of overhead being placed on our Raspberry Pi and the communication link I am changing the control from how the original Max worked. On the original Max you click and drag to set speed and direction. To get that to work as well as it did required the use of queues and threading. While we will continue with some of the threading we will be able to eliminate the queues. In our upgraded MAX2 we will click on the control panel and that one click will set the speed and direction. MAX2 will continue executing that command until we send a change. This potentially causes a problem if the program, running from our PC, crashes or if we lose communication. To handle this problem we will also build in an automatic timer to stop MAX2. We are going to build our control program in modules. You can proceed in the order you like, but I am going to start with a camera module. When possible I am going to make our modules independent so we can run them as stand alone or as import modules.

Pi Camera Module

The goal of this module is to have camera defaults set and to be able to adjust some of the settings from our Python program. In some of my other books I go into more depth on some of the standard modules we will be using, but there is a wealth of information on the web also. After all the imports are coded I set up a camera class. We will create two instances of the class one for display and one to work with. This method makes it a little easier to update the display when changes are made to our variables.

We are also going to create a class for UpdateVideoDisplay. In this class we use labels and buttons for making desired changes. Within this class we also setup a function 'def videoChange(DISP)' to update the Labels of our display. We call this function when we want to update our display.

Because I want this program to run as an import or independently we use the "if __name__ =='__main__':" procedure. If you run the program from a prompt or directly from Geany the program 'knows' to execute the 'main' and the items below it. If we call the program, after importing it, we will call a function of the program. If you are not familiar with this I hope the fog lifts as you work through the program. When you run from the prompt the program will of course do it's normal checking and setup, but it will run the function setupTk(1) as its first step. I have set a switch to indicate where the program is being run from, if run independently I want to set up a normal Tk() window, you may think of it as the root or master window. If run from our control program I want to make the window a Toplevel window; as I do not want to have two master or root windows running.

Under the function 'def startV():' I define the port that we want to send the video to. (You will need to have downloaded Netcat for the Raspberry Pi and the Windows or Linux-Debian PC that you plan to use as your control. You will also need to use a video player on the machine you want to display the video. I am using MPlayer, see appendix for notes on installing that as well and Netcat.) Note the spacing of the commands and the line continuation character '\'. If you have been playing with the camera you may have had some problems stopping the video. As we are using the subprocess function to start the camera we can easily capture it's 'pid', (process identifier). Once we have that we can issue a 'kill' command to stop the process.

If you are running the program from the Raspberry Pi console the video will display on the console, and you will not need Netcat or MPlayer for that purpose. But once we start running remotely you will need them to display your video on the remote PC. Save the program in the same directory that you will place our master control program. I am using /home/pi/MAX3 for all the programs.

When you get to the point of running the program, you will need to start the Netcat program on your PC first. You will see this running in your DOS or command prompt window. Getting Netcat and the MPlayer software running takes some time. You will at some point notice a very noticeable lag between what the camera sees and what is displayed on your screen. This is a result of writing to the cache and reading from the cache. Cache is using a first in first out rule. Try just a short run with the camera on, click stop video, let the cache empty then restart the video. I hope that you get decent results; my delays went away doing this.

I have created an in-depth program to control the Pi Camera. For this book I just put in what I felt we needed as a bare minimum. If you want pretty much complete control of your camera may I self promote another book "Raspberry Pi Camera Controls using Python 3.2.3", the program provided in that book handles STILL and VIDEO, various camera settings and saving pictures to a file. That program is setup like the following one to run standalone or as an import.

```python
1     # Max2 Control Program for camera
2     # using Python 3.2.3    setup to run on Linux
3     # author Herb  11/13/2013 company RyMax, Inc. www.rymax.biz
4     # for personal hobby use only, include references to RyMax Inc. for
5     # resale or commercial use contact RyMax, Inc. for written persmission.
6     from tkinter import *
7     import tkinter.simpledialog
8     import os
9     import subprocess
10    import signal
11    class Camera:
12        def __init__(Data,upDateVideo,videoType,width,height,fps,videoTime,port):
13            Data.upDateVideo=upDateVideo
14            Data.videoType=videoType
15            Data.width=width
16            Data.height=height
17            Data.fps=fps
18            Data.videoTime=videoTime
19            Data.port=port
20    SELF = Camera('video','', 500,400,31,99999,"192.168.1.4 5001")
21    DISP = Camera(' ','', 500, 400, 31,99999,"192.168.1.4 5001")
22    class UpdateVideoDisplay():
23        def __init__(DISP):
24            DISP.vFr = LabelFrame(TOP, width =218, height=218,
25            bd=2, text='Video Setup', relief=GROOVE)
26            DISP.vFr.grid(column =0,row=2,columnspan=3,sticky=(N,E,S))
27            Label(DISP.vFr, text='Current Value').grid(column=0,row=1)
28            Label(DISP.vFr, text='    CLICK to CHANGE').grid(column=1,
29                row=1,sticky=(W))
30            DISP.width = StringVar()
31            DISP.width.set(SELF.width)
32            Label(DISP.vFr,textvariable=DISP.width).grid(column=0,
33                row=2,sticky=(E))
34            Button(DISP.vFr,text="Width",command=imWidth).grid(column=1,
35                row=2,sticky=(W))
36            DISP.height = StringVar()
37            DISP.height.set(SELF.height)
38            Label2=Label(DISP.vFr, textvariable=DISP.height)
39            Label2.grid(column=0, row=3, sticky=(E))
40            Button(DISP.vFr,text="Height",command=imHeight).grid(column=1,
41                row=3,sticky=(W))
42            DISP.fps = StringVar()
43            DISP.fps.set(SELF.fps)
44            Label(DISP.vFr,textvariable=DISP.fps).grid(column=0,
```

Illustration 20

Raspberry Pi Robot with Camera and Sound using Python 3.2   Page 28

```python
45              row=4,sticky=(E))
46          Button(DISP.vFr,text="Frames/Second",command=imfps).grid(column=1,
47              row=4,sticky=(W))
48          DISP.videoTime = StringVar()
49          DISP.videoTime.set(SELF.videoTime)
50          Label(DISP.vFr,textvariable=DISP.videoTime).grid(column=0,
51              row=5,sticky=(E))
52          Button(DISP.vFr,text="Video Time On",command=vTime).grid(column=1,
53              row=5,sticky=(W))
54          DISP.port = StringVar()
55          DISP.port.set(SELF.port)
56          Label(DISP.vFr,textvariable=DISP.port).grid(column=0,
57              row=6,sticky=(E))
58          Button(DISP.vFr,text="Port Select",command=portSelect).grid(column=1,
59              row=6,sticky=(W))
60      def videoChange(DISP):
61          DISP.width.set(SELF.width)
62          DISP.height.set(SELF.height)
63          DISP.fps.set(SELF.fps)
64          DISP.videoTime.set(SELF.videoTime)
65          DISP.port.set(SELF.port)
66  def setupTk(frMain):
67      global TOP
68      if frMain==1:              #program run as stand alone
69          TOP = Tk()
70      if frMain==0:              #program imported & run from other Python script
71          TOP = Toplevel()
72      TOP.title( "Max Camera Center" )
73      TOP.geometry( "240x230+40+490" ) #width, height, placement x  y
74      Button(TOP,text="Run Video",fg='green',command=startV).grid(column=0,
75          row=0,sticky=W)
76      Button(TOP,text="Camera Help",fg='brown',command=helpV).grid(column=1,
77          row=0,sticky=W)
78      Button(TOP,text="STOP VIDEO",fg='red', command=stopV).grid(column=0,
79          row=1,sticky=W)
80      Button(TOP,text="EXIT", fg='red', command=exitCamera).grid(column=1,
81          row=1,sticky=W)
82      UpdateVideoDisplay()
83      SELF.updateVideo=UpdateVideoDisplay()
84  def imWidth():
85      temp=tkinter.simpledialog.askinteger("Enter integer for width",
86          "Between 100 & 1920: ",
87          initialvalue=SELF.width,minvalue=100,maxvalue=1920)
88      if temp != None:
```

Illustration 21

File   Edit   Search   View   Document   Project   Build   Tools   Help

cameraFINAL.py ✖

```
89          │        SELF.width=temp
90          └        SELF.updateVideo.videoChange()
91   ⊟def imHeight():
92    ⊟        temp=tkinter.simpledialog.askinteger("Enter integer for height",
93    │            "Between 50 & 1080: ",
94    ┤            initialvalue=SELF.height,minvalue=50,maxvalue=1080)
95    ⊟        if temp != None:
96    └            SELF.height=temp
97          └        SELF.updateVideo.videoChange()
98   ⊟def imfps():
99    ⊟        temp=tkinter.simpledialog.askinteger("Enter integer for fps",
100   │            "Between 5 & 50:\
101   │            \if you change May need to change nc also",
102   ┤            initialvalue=SELF.fps,minvalue=5,maxvalue=50)
103   ⊟        if temp != None:
104   ┤            SELF.fps=temp
105   └        SELF.updateVideo.videoChange()
106  ⊟def vTime():
107   ⊟        temp=tkinter.simpledialog.askinteger("Integer for Video Time On",
108   │            "Between 999 & 99999999: ",
109   ┤            initialvalue=SELF.videoTime,minvalue=999,maxvalue=99999999)
110   ⊟        if temp != None:
111   ┤            SELF.videoTime=temp
112   └        SELF.updateVideo.videoChange()
113  ⊟def portSelect():
114   ⊟        temp=tkinter.simpledialog.askstring("Enter Port",
115   │            "Example 192.168.1.6 5001",
116   ┤            initialvalue=SELF.port)
117   ⊟        if temp != None:
118   ┤            SELF.port=temp
119   └        SELF.updateVideo.videoChange()
120  ⊟def startV():
121          global p, preexec_fn
122          rPort=' -o - | nc ' +SELF.port
123          camV='raspivid -w '+str(SELF.width)\
124          +' -h '+str(SELF.height)\
125          +' -fps '+str(SELF.fps)\
126          +' -t '+str(SELF.videoTime)\
127          +' -vf --vflip'\
128          +' -hf --hflip'\
129          + rPort
130          p = subprocess.Popen(camV, shell=True, preexec_fn=os.setsid )
131          print ('Child PID: ', p.pid)
132   └        print (camV)
```

line: 111 / 149   col: 25   sel: 0   INS   TAB   mode: Win (CRLF)   encoding: UTF-8   filetype: Python   scope: vTime

Illustration 22

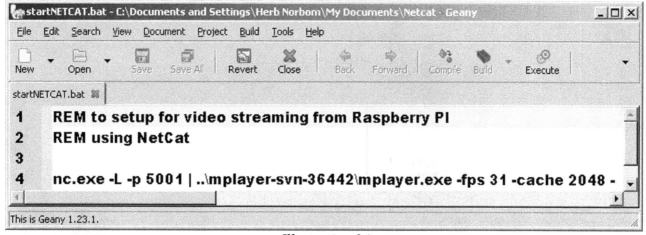

```
cameraFINAL.py - /home/pi/MAX3 - Geany

File  Edit  Search  View  Document  Project  Build  Tools  Help

cameraFINAL.py

133  def exitCamera():
134       global p, preexec_fn
135       try:
136           os.killpg(p.pid, signal.SIGTERM)
137       except:
138           pass
139       TOP.destroy()
140  def stopV():
141       global p, preexec_fn
142       os.killpg(p.pid, signal.SIGTERM)
143  def helpV():
144       camV='raspivid -? &'
145       subprocess.Popen(camV, shell=True )
146  if __name__ == '__main__':
147       setupTk(1)
148       mainloop()
149

line: 111 / 149  col: 25  sel: 0   INS   TAB   mode: Win (CRLF)   encoding: UTF-8   filetype: Python   scope: vTime
```

Illustration 23

On the Windows PC I set up the following bat file to start Netcat and MPlayer. I saved Netcat and MPlayer in My Documents directory. To run them I set up a batch file in the 'netcat' directory. See the Appendix for instructions on downloading Netcat and MPlayer. The following is the simple bat file I created to get it running. You can setup a similar script on the Debian-Linux PC if you like, remember to make it executable.

```
startNETCAT.bat - C:\Documents and Settings\Herb Norbom\My Documents\Netcat - Geany

File  Edit  Search  View  Document  Project  Build  Tools  Help

New    Open    Save   Save All   Revert   Close    Back  Forward   Compile  Build   Execute

startNETCAT.bat

1   REM to setup for video streaming from Raspberry PI
2   REM using NetCat
3
4   nc.exe -L -p 5001 | ..\mplayer-svn-36442\mplayer.exe -fps 31 -cache 2048 -

This is Geany 1.23.1.
```

Illustration 24

Play Wav Files

I have added speakers to my robot and the Raspberry Pi makes it pretty easy to use them. The following program is build very similar to the camera program. I want to be able to run this program independently or as an import. Before you get into the program I suggest you get your speakers working. I had some problems in this area; see the Appendix for how I got the speakers working. I found a small pair of speakers at one of the discount stores for a couple of bucks that had a battery amplifier built-in. Or go wild, you can buy or build a small amplifier or add speakers that need another power supply. Needless to say lots of choices. The speakers shown run on two AAA batteries. This program will only play 'wav' files. The system program 'aplay' does not play all wav files. The files need to be 'PCM or float enabled' to work. There are ways to convert the wav file, search the web as I am not going to cover that here. As I want to be able to choose a wav file from what I have stored on the disk I set up a separate directory up one level from where the program is saved. My directory for the wav files is "/home/pi/mysounds". I also used the tkinter listbox capabilities to display the wav files in the directory and for the actual selection. Save the program in the same directory that you will place our master control program. I am using /home/pi/MAX3 for all the programs.

```
musicWavPlayFINAL.py - /home/pi/MAX3 - Geany

File  Edit  Search  View  Document  Project  Build  Tools  Help

musicWavPlayFINAL.py

1    # Max2 Control Program   play wav file
2    # using Python 3.2.3    setup to run on Linux
3    # author Herb  11/14/2013  company RyMax, Inc. www.rymax.biz
4    # for personal hobby use only, include references to RyMax Inc. for
5    # resale or commercial use contact RyMax, Inc. for written persmission.
6    from tkinter import *
7    import os
8
9    def on_click_listbox(event):
10       index = soundBox.curselection()    # get selected line index
11       soundFile = soundBox.get(index)    # get the line's text
12       label1.configure(text=soundFile)   # show slected text in label
13       path='../mysounds/'
14       if soundFile != None:
15           extension = os.path.splitext(soundFile)[1][1:]
16           print (extension)
17           selected='aplay '+path+soundFile
18           print (selected)
19           if ((extension=='wav') | (extension=='WAV')):
20               os.system(selected)
21
22    def setupTk():
23       global soundBox, label1
24       TOP = Tk()
25       TOP.title( "Max Sound Center" )
26       TOP.geometry( "200x200+550+130" ) #width, height, placement x  y
27    #list box wav list
28       soundFrame = LabelFrame(TOP, text="Max Sounds",width=20,
29           height=10,cursor="arrow")
30       soundFrame.grid(column=0, row =2, sticky=(N,W,S))

line: 50 / 50    col: 0    sel: 0    INS    TAB    mode: Win (CRLF)    encoding: UTF-8    filetype: Python    scope: setupTk
```

Illustration 25

```
31        soundBox=Listbox(soundFrame, width=20, height=8)
32        soundBox.grid(column=0,row=1,sticky=(N,W,S))
33        scrollBar = Scrollbar(soundFrame, orient=VERTICAL, command=soundBox.yview)
34        scrollBar.grid(column=1,row=1, sticky=(N,E,S))
35        soundBox['yscrollcommand']=scrollBar.set
36        path='../mysounds'
37        soundlist = os.listdir(path)
38        Button(soundFrame, text="EXIT", fg='red',command=TOP.destroy).grid(column=0,row=4)
39    # load the listbox
40        for sound in soundlist:
41            extension = os.path.splitext(sound)[1][1:]
42            if ((extension=='wav') | (extension=='WAV')):
43                soundBox.insert('end', sound)
44        label1 = Label(soundFrame, text='click to play', width=20, bg='white')
45        label1.grid(column=0, row=0)
46        soundBox.bind('<ButtonRelease-1>', on_click_listbox)
47    if __name__ == '__main__':
48        setupTk()
49        mainloop()
50
```

Illustration 26

Illustration 27

Text to Speech

Max likes to read prepared speech, much like robotic government officials. I could not get the teleprompter to work very well with Max, he keeps trying to drive over it, while he mutters something about Washington. Anyway, Python has some great capabilities in this area also; you will however need to download 'eSpeak'. See the Appendix for download and install instructions.

This program like our first two programs is setup to run independently or as an import. The program has an input box for giving Max the ability to go 'off record' and get it trouble by himself. I found with eSpeak that I had to write the text to a file and then read the file rather than reading a variable. Not sure why, but as I created some text files and saved them in the same directory as the music, not really a problem.

You may have noticed that our programs open in separate areas of your display. I have tried to place them so all can be open at once along with our soon to be written master control program. You may need or want to adjust the positions depending on your display. Or you can just grab them and place as you like when they are opened. When you run this program there is a lot of information displayed on your monitor that is not necessary. There is probably a way to turn it off or redirect it to a temp file. While a little annoying it is not a problem so I just ignore it. Save the program in the same directory that you will place our master control program. I am using /home/pi/MAX3 for all the programs.

File   Edit   Search   View   Document   Project   Build   Tools   Help

speakTextFINAL.py ✖

```
 1      # Max2 Control Program   Text to Voice
 2      # using Python 3.2.3    setup to run on Linux
 3      # author Herb  11/14/2013  company RyMax, Inc. www.rymax.biz
 4      # for personal hobby use only, include references to RyMax Inc. for
 5      # resale or commercial use contact RyMax, Inc. for written persmission.
 6      from tkinter import *
 7      import tkinter.simpledialog
 8      import os
 9
10      def maxSpeak():
11          whatToSay=tkinter.simpledialog.askstring("Text for Max","Enter what to say")
12          print(whatToSay)
13          if ((whatToSay=="") | (whatToSay==None)):   #cancel returns None
14              return
15          try:
16              with open("temp.txt","w") as f:
17                  f.write(whatToSay)
18          except:
19              print ('Error writing to temp.txt in current directory')
20          engageSpeech()
21      def engageSpeech():
22          try:
23              with open("temp.txt","r") as f:
24                  myFile=f.read()
25                  print (myFile)
26                  os.system('espeak -ven -k9 -p10 -s200 -f temp.txt')
27          except:
28              print ('error on speaking')
29      def on_click_listbox(event):
30          index = soundBox.curselection()      # get selected line index
31          soundFile = soundBox.get(index)      # get the line's text
32          label1.configure(text=soundFile)     # show slected text in label
33          path='../mysounds/'
34          if soundFile != None:
35              extension = os.path.splitext(soundFile)[1][1:]
36              print (extension)
37              if((extension=='text') | (extension=='txt')):
38                  mpath= "../mysounds/"+soundFile
39                  print (mpath)
40                  try:
41                      with open(mpath,"r") as f:
42                          myFile=f.read()
```

line: 83 / 83   col: 0   sel: 0   INS   TAB   MOD   mode: Win (CRLF)   encoding: UTF-8   filetype: Python   scope: unknown

Illustration 28

```
43              print (myFile)
44          except:
45              print ("Error reading text file")
46          try:
47              with open("temp.txt","w") as f:
48                  print (myFile)
49                  f.write(myFile)
50          except:
51              print ('Error writing to temp.txt in current directory')
52          engageSpeech()
53  def setupTk():
54      global soundBox, label1
55      TOP = Tk()
56      TOP.title( "Max Control Center" )
57      TOP.geometry( "200x200+760+130" ) #width, height, placement x  y
58      bFrame = LabelFrame(TOP,width=100, height=15)
59      bFrame.grid(column=0,columnspan=4, row=0, sticky=(N,W,S))
60      Button(bFrame, text = "MAXSPEAK", fg="white",
61      command = maxSpeak).grid(column=0, row=0)
62      soundFrame = LabelFrame(TOP, text="Max Sounds",width=20, height=10,cursor="arrow")
63      soundFrame.grid(column=0, row =2, sticky=(N,W,S))
64      soundBox=Listbox(soundFrame, width=20, height=7)
65      soundBox.grid(column=0,row=1,sticky=(N,W,S))
66      scrollBar = Scrollbar(soundFrame, orient=VERTICAL, command=soundBox.yview)
67      scrollBar.grid(column=1,row=1, sticky=(N,E,S))
68      soundBox['yscrollcommand']=scrollBar.set
69      path='../mysounds'
70      soundlist = os.listdir(path)
71      Button(soundFrame, text="EXIT", fg='red',command=TOP.destroy).grid(column=0,row=4)
72  # load the listbox
73      for sound in soundlist:
74          extension = os.path.splitext(sound)[1][1:]
75          if ((extension=='txt') | (extension=='TXT') |(extension=='text')):
76              soundBox.insert('end', sound)
77      label1 = Label(soundFrame, text='click to play', width=20, bg='white')
78      label1.grid(column=0, row=0)
79      soundBox.bind('<ButtonRelease-1>', on_click_listbox)
80  if __name__ == '__main__':
81      setupTk()
82      mainloop()
```

line: 83 / 83   col: 0   sel: 0   INS   TAB   MOD   mode: Win (CRLF)   encoding: UTF-8   filetype: Python   scope: unknown

Illustration 29

Servo Move Head

Before we get to the master control program I want to go over one more module. Max wants to be able to move his head. For this only about 180°, close to what we can turn our heads, but this is only left and right. The platform uses a Parallax Standard Servo(#900-00005). To support the platform I am using the inner plastic ring that supports the glass plate from an old micro wave oven. That ring sits on the platform that the servo is mounted on. On top of the ring sits another platform with a base that slides over the servo armature. In my case it is not a tight fit. On this platform I have mounted a board that holds the Pi, the Pi camera and my board for regulating the voltage. (For Max's next upgrade I will go to a lighter head, a more powerful servo or maybe a stepper motor. While this works for me it is not that great.) Over all of this I gave Max a good looking head made from the lid of a small garbage can. I cut the flap a little on both ends so Max could see and to allow easier access for all the wires. The wiring for the servo is pretty straight forward. There are three wires, the red wire needs +5 volts, the black wire goes to ground. The white wire is for the actual control. The servo's position is controlled by pulse power using specific timing. Sounds like a PWM application to me, and it is. Just be aware that in using the Pi and Python we are not going to get real precision. There are other actions taking place in the Pi and with Python that can impact timing, but you could say Max just has a crook in his neck. To get the timing you can go through the following steps to see the reasoning. I am not overclocking the Pi, just plain vanilla for me. A good reference site is "A Slice of Raspberry Pi" http://asliceofraspberrypi.blogspot.com/2013/05/displaying-system-information-and.html. The site has good information, I am not recommending that you change the clock speed of your Pi, just see what it is. At the prompt enter "vcgencmd measure_clock arm" . This should return "frequency(45)=700000000". This is nice to know, but we are going to be using the Python time.sleep function. The time.sleep function uses seconds. For my servo I need a time between pulses of 20 milliseconds. A millisecond, ms = 1/1000 of a second. So if we do the math 1/1000*20 we get 0.02 seconds. In using the servo data sheet I see that full right is 0.00225, full left is 0.00075 and center is 0.0015. Positions between full left or full right just use numbers that fall within the range limits. You may need to play with the numbers some to get it working to your satisfaction.

To help get the setting correct or at least working I set up the class 'headMove'. By using a class it is easy to change all the variables from one location. I also have set the program up so it can be imported or run as standalone. While we are using PWM I found setting the power or Duty Cycle at 100 worked best. I also built a time delay in so the head did not spin too quickly. With the timing not being perfect a return to center became a little bit of a challenge. I finally just setup some limits and if the head moved to a point within them I would stop adjusting.

The tkinter window has buttons to go full left or right as well as to center. Also we have buttons to step to right or left along with our EXIT button.

```
 1    # Max2 Control Program   move head using servo
 2    # using Python 3.2.3   setup to run on Linux
 3    # author Herb  11/14/2013  company RyMax, Inc. www.rymax.biz
 4    # for personal hobby use only, include references to RyMax Inc. for
 5    # resale or commercial use contact RyMax, Inc. for written persmission.
 6    from tkinter import *
 7    #import os
 8    import RPi.GPIO as GPIO      #set the mode for numbering the pins
 9    GPIO.setmode(GPIO.BOARD)     # Using BOARD.GPIO
10    from time import sleep
11    import time
12    class headMove:
13        def __init__(Data,limitRight,limitLeft,limitCenter,pCurrent,p12,power,
14            msTime,delayT,incrementMove):
15            Data.limitRight=limitRight
16            Data.limitLeft=limitLeft
17            Data.limitCenter=limitCenter
18            Data.pCurrent=pCurrent
19            Data.p12=p12
20            Data.power=power
21            Data.msTime=msTime
22            Data.delayT=delayT
23            Data.incrementMove=incrementMove
24        def controlPins(Data):
25            print ('at setup controlPins')
26            GPIO.setup(12, GPIO.OUT)
27            Data.p12=GPIO.PWM(12, 50)        #try various frequencies
28            GPIO.setup(12, GPIO.IN)       #setup and turn off
```

Illustration 30

File   Edit   Search   View   Document   Project   Build   Tools   Help

moveHeadFINAL.py ✖

```python
29  HEAD = headMove(0.00225,              #Servo limitRight
30                  0.00075,              #Servo limitLeft
31                  0.0015,               #Servo limitCenter
32                  0.0015,               #Servo current postion
33                  ' ',                  #start to setup GPIO pin12
34                  100,                  #power value or Duty Cycle
35                  0.02,                 #setting to get approx 20ms for servo 1/1000*20
36                  0.2,                  #delay to slow down the movement
37                  0.00005)              #increment move amount
38  def moveFullRight():
39      while HEAD.pCurrent > HEAD.limitLeft:
40          print ('moveRight current position ', HEAD.pCurrent, ' limit: ',HEAD.limitLeft)
41          HEAD.p12.start(HEAD.power)
42          GPIO.setup(12, GPIO.OUT)
43          time.sleep(HEAD.pCurrent)
44          GPIO.setup(12, GPIO.IN)
45          time.sleep(HEAD.msTime)                #20ms
46          HEAD.pCurrent=HEAD.pCurrent-HEAD.incrementMove
47          time.sleep(HEAD.delayT)                #short delay to slow down movement
48      HEAD.p12.start(0)                          #set power level to zero
49  def moveRight():
50      if HEAD.pCurrent > HEAD.limitLeft:
51          print ('moveRight current position ', HEAD.pCurrent, ' limit: ',HEAD.limitLeft)
52          HEAD.p12.start(HEAD.power)
53          GPIO.setup(12, GPIO.OUT)
54          time.sleep(HEAD.pCurrent)
55          GPIO.setup(12, GPIO.IN)
56          time.sleep(HEAD.msTime)                #20ms
57          HEAD.pCurrent=HEAD.pCurrent-HEAD.incrementMove
58      HEAD.p12.start(0)                          #set power level to zero
59  def moveCenter():
60      Center=1
61      while Center:
62          print ('atmoveCenter & limit', HEAD.pCurrent,' ',HEAD.limitCenter)
63          testDiff = HEAD.pCurrent - HEAD.limitCenter
64          time.sleep(HEAD.delayT)                #short delay to slow down movement
65          if testDiff >=-.0001 and testDiff <=.0001:
66              HEAD.p12.start(HEAD.power)
67              GPIO.setup(12, GPIO.OUT)
68              time.sleep(HEAD.limitCenter)  #final adjust to position
69              GPIO.setup(12, GPIO.IN)
70              print ('at end center')
71              break
72              Center=0
```

line: 6 / 140   col: 6   sel: 0   INS   TAB   mode: Win (CRLF)   encoding: UTF-8   filetype: Python   scope: unknown

Illustration 31

```
73         if HEAD.pCurrent > HEAD.limitCenter:
74             HEAD.p12.start(HEAD.power)
75             GPIO.setup(12, GPIO.OUT)
76             time.sleep(HEAD.pCurrent)
77             GPIO.setup(12, GPIO.IN)
78             time.sleep(HEAD.msTime)
79             HEAD.pCurrent=HEAD.pCurrent -HEAD.incrementMove
80         else:
81             HEAD.p12.start(HEAD.power)
82             GPIO.setup(12, GPIO.OUT)
83             time.sleep(HEAD.pCurrent)
84             GPIO.setup(12, GPIO.IN)
85             time.sleep(HEAD.msTime)
86             HEAD.pCurrent=HEAD.pCurrent +HEAD.incrementMove
87     HEAD.p12.start(0)                    #set power level to zero
88 def moveFullLeft():
89     while HEAD.pCurrent < HEAD.limitRight:
90         print ('moveLeft current position ', HEAD.pCurrent,' limit: ',HEAD.limitRight)
91         HEAD.p12.start(HEAD.power)
92         GPIO.setup(12, GPIO.OUT)
93         time.sleep(HEAD.pCurrent)
94         GPIO.setup(12, GPIO.IN)
95         time.sleep(HEAD.msTime)
96         HEAD.pCurrent=HEAD.pCurrent+HEAD.incrementMove
97         time.sleep(HEAD.delayT)              #short delay to slow down movement
98     HEAD.p12.start(0)                    #set power level to zero
99 def moveLeft():
100    if HEAD.pCurrent < HEAD.limitRight:
101        print ('moveLeft current position ', HEAD.pCurrent,' limit: ',HEAD.limitRight)
102        HEAD.p12.start(HEAD.power)
103        GPIO.setup(12, GPIO.OUT)
104        time.sleep(HEAD.pCurrent)
105        GPIO.setup(12, GPIO.IN)
106        time.sleep(HEAD.msTime)
107        HEAD.pCurrent=HEAD.pCurrent+HEAD.incrementMove
108    HEAD.p12.start(0)                    #set power level to zero
109 def callEXIT():
110    global TOP
111    print("program stop ordered")           # display on console
112    HEAD.p12.start(0)                    #set power level to zero
113    try:
114        GPIO.cleanup()
115        print ('GPIO has been stopped and cleaned')
116        TOP.destroy()            #close tkinter windows
```

Illustration 32

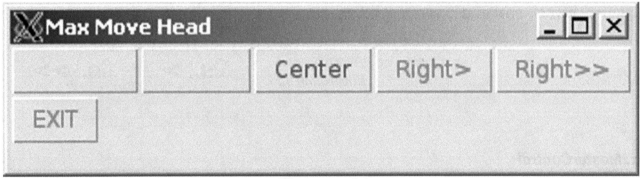

```
117    except:
118        print ('error stop or clean GPIO')
119 def setupTk(frMain):
120    global TOP
121    if frMain==1:              #program run as stand alone
122        TOP = Tk()
123    if frMain==0:              #program imported and run from different Python script
124        TOP = Toplevel()
125    TOP.title( "Max Move Head" )
126    TOP.geometry( "340x65+550+30" ) #width, height, placement x  y
127    Button(TOP, text="<< Left", fg='green',command=moveFullLeft).grid(column=1, row=1)
128    Button(TOP, text="< Left", fg='green',command=moveLeft).grid(column=2, row=1)
129    Button(TOP, text="Center", fg='blue',command=moveCenter).grid(column=3, row=1)
130    Button(TOP, text="Right>", fg='red',command=moveRight).grid(column=4, row=1)
131    Button(TOP, text="Right>>", fg='red',command=moveFullRight).grid(column=5, row=1)
132    if frMain==1:
133        Button(TOP, text="EXIT", fg='red',command=callEXIT).grid(column=1,
134            row=4,sticky=(W))
135    headMove.controlPins(HEAD)          #define GPIO pins
136    HEAD.p12.start(0)                   #set power level to zero
137 if __name__ == '__main__':
138    setupTk(1)
139    mainloop()
```

Illustration 33

Illustration 34

In the following diagram for the servo I have included the Front Bumper, which we activate in the next program. This diagram includes all the wiring that we need for our robot; except for the battery supply to power the Pi. Also, while not shown, add a switch to turn the power off and on.

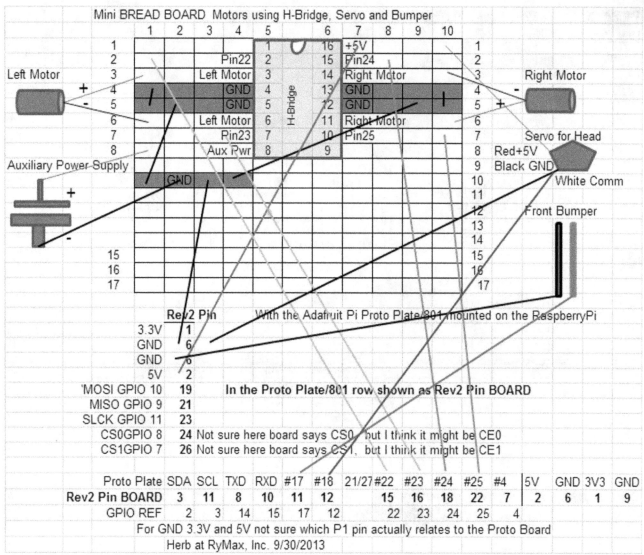

Illustration 35

Herb at RyMax, Inc. 9/30/2013

Rev2 Pin		
3.3V	1	
GND	6	
GND	6	
5V	2	
'MOSI GPIO 10	19	
MISO GPIO 9	21	
SLCK GPIO 11	23	
CS0GPIO 8	24	Not sure here board says CS0, but I think it might be CE0
CS1GPIO 7	26	Not sure here board says CS1, but I think it might be CE1

In the Proto Plate/801 row shown as Rev2 Pin BOARD

Proto Plate	SDA	SCL	TXD	RXD	#17	#18	21/27	#22	#23	#24	#25	#4	5V	GND	3V3	GND
Rev2 Pin BOARD	3	11	8	10	11	12		15	16	18	22	7	2	6	1	9
GPIO REF	2	3	14	15	17	12		22	23	24	25	4				

For GND 3.3V and 5V not sure which P1 pin actually relates to the Proto Board

Max2MasterControl

This will be our main program and it will have the capabilities needed to control our robot and to import and run the first four programs. While we do begin to setup the GPIO capabilities in this program I split the actual motor control into a separate module. Hopefully this will make the module more useful as Max continues to improve. This program does get into some of Python's more complicated areas, such as using 'subprocess' and 'threading'. In my first book on Max I went into a fair amount of depth in those areas. I am not going to repeat all of that 'stuff'; you can do more research on line. I will give you the basic 'stuff' that you need. We are also going to import the modules we wrote for the camera, playing a wav file, text to speech and servo control. You can of course leave any of those modules out if you so desire.

I setup the class 'UpdateDisplay' to give us our basic screen display. We want to use a class because it allows us to easily update the displayed information. Plus it just helps with our program organization.

Our next section is the meat of the program. In this section we capture the click of the mouse on the screen to compute the direction and speed for Max. There are of course a lot of ways to do this. I will attempt to explain my reasoning and provide a short diagram to help visualize it. The display screen can be thought of as having thousands of little boxes (or pixels) that are arranged in x number of vertical columns and y number of horizontal rows. The combination of x and y numbers point to a position on the display screen. The numbering starts in the top left hand corner of the display screen. The numbers are shown in pairs, with the x value shown first "(x,y)". So the very top left most position is (0,0). Over to the right 10 positions and down 15 positions would be (10,15). I am using a small subsection of the display screen for controlling Max's movement. I define this section in the "setupCanvas" function. To calculate the direction and speed I want to set the middle of the canvas to (0,0) without changing a lot. To do this when I setup the function "paint" I take my mouse event and subtract values that I have determined will adjust the mouse event to the center of my "Canvas". As you can see the canvas width 270 and the height is 210. One half of the size gives us the center. Now I think of our canvas as having four quadrants.

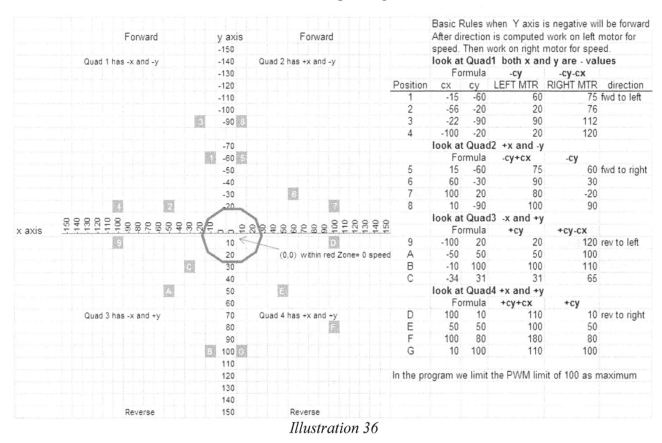

Basic Rules when Y axis is negative will be forward
After direction is computed work on left motor for speed. Then work on right motor for speed.

look at Quad1 both x and y are - values

Position	cx	cy	LEFT MTR	RIGHT MTR	direction
			Formula -cy	-cy-cx	
1	-15	-60	60	75	fwd to left
2	-56	-20	20	76	
3	-22	-90	90	112	
4	-100	-20	20	120	

look at Quad2 +x and -y

Position	cx	cy	LEFT MTR	RIGHT MTR	direction
			Formula -cy+cx	-cy	
5	15	-60	75	60	fwd to right
6	60	-30	90	30	
7	100	20	80	-20	
8	10	-90	100	90	

look at Quad3 -x and +y

Position	cx	cy	LEFT MTR	RIGHT MTR	direction
			Formula +cy	+cy-cx	
9	-100	20	20	120	rev to left
A	-50	50	50	100	
B	-10	100	100	110	
C	-34	31	31	65	

look at Quad4 +x and +y

Position	cx	cy	LEFT MTR	RIGHT MTR	direction
			Formula +cy+cx	+cy	
D	100	10	110	10	rev to right
E	50	50	100	50	
F	100	80	180	80	
G	10	100	110	100	

In the program we limit the PWM limit of 100 as maximum

Illustration 36

As you can see from the quadrants illustration a value can exceed 100 which is the maximum PWM value, so a logic limit of 100 is included.

I have added a fair amount of 'print' statements, most of these are here just to help debug the program, they are not needed from an operational viewpoint.

Threading is used for two functions. The first one is for updating our display panel. You can adjust the timing for the refreshing or updating by changing the time.sleep function. The second thread is for running a timer that I use as a fail safe stop the robot routine. When we send a movement signal to Max he will keep executing that command until we send another. My concern is that if communication is lost or my PC goes down Max would continue on his last mission. I use a thread to start a counter, the counter goes for 3-5 seconds and if a command is not received a STOP all motors is executed. I have also included a front bumper to stop Max; I felt this fail safe was also important. Without going into detail on the threads you need to set all child threads before starting any of them. Set the Daemon to True so that when you close the window the threads are automatically stopped.   Go ahead and enter the program,'max2ControlFINAL.py', sorry it will not work until you also code the next module for GPIO control.

```
max2ControlFINAL.py - /home/pi/MAX3 - Geany                                    _ |□| X
File  Edit  Search  View  Document  Project  Build  Tools  Help

max2ControlFINAL.py ✖  max2Module3FINAL.py ✖

 1    # Max2 Control Program  using Python 3.2.3    setup to run on Linux
 2    # author Herb  11/12/2013  company RyMax, Inc. www.rymax.biz
 3    # for personal hobby use only, include references to RyMax Inc. for
 4    # resale or commercial use contact RyMax, Inc. for written persmission.
 5    from tkinter import *
 6    import tkinter.messagebox
 7    import subprocess
 8    from time import sleep
 9    import time
10    import threading
11    from threading import Thread
12    import RPi.GPIO as GPIO      #set mode pin numbering. We are using BOARD GPIO
13    GPIO.setmode(GPIO.BOARD)
14    gpioversion=GPIO.BOARD                      #for Information only
15    print ('GPIO Board version: ',gpioversion)
16    gpioversion2=GPIO.VERSION                    #for Information only
17    print ('GPIO Version2: ' ,gpioversion2)
18    gpioRevision =GPIO.RPI_REVISION              #for Information only
19    print ('GPIO Revision: ', gpioRevision)
20
21    import musicWavPlayFINAL
22    import max2Module3FINAL as MOTOR
23    import speakTextFINAL
24    import cameraFINAL
25    import moveHeadFINAL
26
27    class UpdateDisplay:                    #display messages
28        def __init__(DISP, root):
29            DISP.robotFrame = LabelFrame(root, text="**Left Motor     **Right Motor**")
30            DISP.robotFrame.config(width=25, cursor="arrow")
31            DISP.robotFrame.grid(column=1, row =3, sticky=(N,W))
32
33            DISP.Left = Label(DISP.robotFrame, text="LEFT MOTOR")
34            DISP.Left.grid(column=0,row=1,sticky=(N,W,E,S))
35            DISP.Right = Label(DISP.robotFrame, text="RIGHT MOTOR")
36            DISP.Right.grid(column=1,row=1,sticky=(N,W,E,S))
37
38            DISP.LeftMtrDir = StringVar()
39            DISP.LeftMtrDir.set(MOTOR.MTR.LeftMtrDir)
40            DISP.msgRec = Label(DISP.robotFrame, textvariable=DISP.LeftMtrDir)
41            DISP.msgRec.grid(column=0,row=1,sticky=(N,W,E,S))
42
43            DISP.RightMtrDir = StringVar()
44            DISP.RightMtrDir.set(MOTOR.MTR.RightMtrDir)

line: 6 / 258    col: 25    sel: 0    INS    TAB    mode: Win (CRLF)    encoding: UTF-8    filetype: Python    scope: unknown
```

Illustration 37

max2ControlFINAL.py - /home/pi/MAX3 - Geany
File   Edit   Search   View   Document   Project   Build   Tools   Help
max2ControlFINAL.py   max2Module3FINAL.py

```
45            DISP.msgRec = Label(DISP.robotFrame, textvariable=DISP.RightMtrDir)
46            DISP.msgRec.grid(column=1,row=1,sticky=(N,W,E,S))
47
48            DISP.LeftDC = StringVar()
49            DISP.LeftDC.set(MOTOR.MTR.displayLeftDC)
50            DISP.msgSend = Label(DISP.robotFrame, textvariable=DISP.LeftDC)
51            DISP.msgSend.grid(column=0,row=2,sticky=(N,W,E,S))
52
53            DISP.RightDC = StringVar()
54            DISP.RightDC.set(MOTOR.MTR.displayRightDC)
55            DISP.msgSend = Label(DISP.robotFrame, textvariable=DISP.RightDC)
56            DISP.msgSend.grid(column=1,row=2,sticky=(N,W,E,S))
57
58            DISP.systemMsg= StringVar()
59            DISP.systemMsg.set(MOTOR.MTR.sysMsg)
60            DISP.sysMsg = Label(DISP.robotFrame, textvariable=DISP.systemMsg)
61            DISP.sysMsg.grid(column=0,columnspan=2,row=3, sticky=(N,W,E,S))
62
63      def msgFromMax(DISP):
64            DISP.LeftMtrDir.set(MOTOR.MTR.LeftMtrDir)
65            DISP.RightMtrDir.set(MOTOR.MTR.RightMtrDir)
66            DISP.LeftDC.set(MOTOR.MTR.displayLeftDC)
67            DISP.RightDC.set(MOTOR.MTR.displayRightDC)
68            DISP.systemMsg.set(MOTOR.MTR.sysMsg)
69
70   def paint( event ):
71        print ('at paint')
72        cx=cy=0
73        try:
74            cx=(event.x-135)              #set cx to center of canvas
75            cy=(event.y-105)              #set cy to center of canvas
76            print ('cx= ',cx,'   cy= ',cy)
77        except:
78            cx=0                          # if something not working want to
79            cy=0                          # set mouse event location to (0,0)
80   #determine direction and speed
81        MOTOR.MTR.myFailSafe=0                    #reset counter
82        if ((-10 <=cy<=10) and (-10<=cx<=10)):            #stop area
83            print ('at stop')
84            MOTOR.stopAll()
85            return
86
87        if ((cy <= 0)&(cx<=0)):               #forward in Quad1
88            print ('forward Quad1')
```

Illustration 38

Raspberry Pi Robot with Camera and Sound using Python 3.2   Page 45

```
 89            MOTOR.MTR.LeftMtrDir="FWD"
 90            MOTOR.MTR.RightMtrDir="FWD"
 91            if ((cx <= 0) & (cy<=0)):                    #left turn
 92                tempLeftDC=(-cy)                         #left motor Quad1
 93                if tempLeftDC>100:
 94                    tempLeftDC=100
 95                MOTOR.MTR.LeftDC=tempLeftDC
 96                print ('Left Motor fwd DC= ', MOTOR.MTR.LeftDC)
 97                tempRightDC=(-cy-cx)                        #right motor Quad1
 98                if tempRightDC>100:
 99                    tempRightDC=100
100                MOTOR.MTR.RightDC=tempRightDC
101                print ('Right Motor fwd DC= ',MOTOR.MTR.RightDC)
102            MOTOR.MTR.displayRightDC=MOTOR.MTR.RightDC
103            MOTOR.MTR.displayLeftDC=MOTOR.MTR.LeftDC
104            MOTOR.fwd()
105            return
106        if ((cx > 0) & (cy<0)):                  #forward in Quad2
107            print ('forward Quad2')
108            MOTOR.MTR.LeftMtrDir="FWD"
109            MOTOR.MTR.RightMtrDir="FWD"
110            tempLeftDC=(-cy+cx)                      #left motor Quad2
111            if tempLeftDC>100:
112                tempLeftDC=100
113            MOTOR.MTR.LeftDC=tempLeftDC
114            print ('Left Motor fwd DC= ', MOTOR.MTR.LeftDC)
115            tempRightDC=(-cy)                        #right motor Quad2
116            if tempRightDC>100:
117                tempRightDC=100
118            MOTOR.MTR.RightDC=tempRightDC
119            print ('Right Motor fwd DC= ',MOTOR.MTR.RightDC)
120            MOTOR.MTR.displayRightDC=MOTOR.MTR.RightDC
121            MOTOR.MTR.displayLeftDC=MOTOR.MTR.LeftDC
122            MOTOR.fwd()
123            return
124
125        if (cy >=0)&(cx<=0):                         #reverse  in Quad3
126            print ('reverse Quad3')
127            MOTOR.MTR.LeftMtrDir='REV'
128            MOTOR.MTR.RightMtrDir='REV'
129            if cx <0:                               #left turn in reverse Quad3
130                tempLeftDC=(+cy)                     #left motor
131                if tempLeftDC>100:
132                    tempLeftDC=100
```

Illustration 39

Raspberry Pi Robot with Camera and Sound using Python 3.2   Page 46

```
133                         MOTOR.MTR.LeftDC=tempLeftDC
134                         print ('Left turn rev Left Motor= ',MOTOR.MTR.LeftDC)
135                     tempRightDC=(+cy-cx)          #set right motor power
136             if tempRightDC>100:
137                     tempRightDC=100
138                 MOTOR.MTR.RightDC=tempRightDC
139                 print ('Left turn rev Right Motor= ',MOTOR.MTR.RightDC)
140                 MOTOR.MTR.displayRightDC=MOTOR.MTR.RightDC
141                 MOTOR.MTR.displayLeftDC=MOTOR.MTR.LeftDC
142                 MOTOR.rev()
143                 return
144
145         if ((cx >0)&(cy>0)):                      #right turn in reverse Quad4
146                 print ('reverse Quad4')
147                 MOTOR.MTR.LeftMtrDir='REV'
148                 MOTOR.MTR.RightMtrDir='REV'
149                 tempLeftDC=(+cy+cx)          #left motor
150             if tempLeftDC>100:
151                     tempLeftDC=100
152                 MOTOR.MTR.LeftDC=tempLeftDC
153                 print ('Left turn rev Left Motor= ',MOTOR.MTR.LeftDC)
154                 tempRightDC=(+cy)          #set right motor power
155             if tempRightDC>100:
156                     tempRightDC=100
157                 MOTOR.MTR.RightDC=tempRightDC
158                 print ('Left turn rev Right Motor= ',MOTOR.MTR.RightDC)
159                 MOTOR.MTR.displayRightDC=MOTOR.MTR.RightDC
160                 MOTOR.MTR.displayLeftDC=MOTOR.MTR.LeftDC
161                 MOTOR.rev()
162                 return
163
164     def callEXIT():
165         MOTOR.stopAll()
166         print("program stop ordered")          # display on console
167         MOTOR.MTR.sysMsg='Exit called'              # display on message pannel
168         answer=tkinter.messagebox.askyesno("EXIT", "Do you really want to quit")
169         if answer==True:
170             try:
171                 GPIO.cleanup()
172                 print ('GPIO has been stopped and cleaned')
173             except:
174                 print ('error stop or clean GPIO')
175             try:
176                 root.quit() #closes all windows
```

Illustration 40

```
177                        #stops threads because daemon set, will get occasional
178                        #error as thread tries to write, but function closing
179                        #if this is a problem make the except a 'pass'
180      except:
181            print ('error on quit')
182
183  def setupCanvas():
184      myCanvas = Canvas( root, width =270, height=210, bd=2, relief=GROOVE )
185      myCanvas.grid(column=1,row=0,columnspan=2,sticky=(N,W))
186      myCanvas.configure(cursor="crosshair")
187      myCanvas.bind( "<Button-1>", paint )
188      myCanvas.create_line(4, 105, 268, 105, width=1)#  horizontal
189      myCanvas.create_line(135,  4, 135, 208, width=1)# vertical
190      myCanvas.create_rectangle(125,95,145,115, fill='red')#click box to stop
191
192  def wavPlayer():
193      musicWavPlayFINAL.setupTk()
194  def txtPlayer():
195      speakTextFINAL.setupTk()
196  def cameraSetup():
197      cameraFINAL.setupTk(0)
198  def displayStaticStuff():
199      Label( root, text = "Click RED BOX to stop, Click With Cross Hair to move",
200      font=("Helvetica",8)).grid( column=0, row =1,columnspan=4,stick=(N,W,E,S))
201      robotStatusframe = LabelFrame(root, text="Max2 Status",width=20,
202      height=5,cursor="arrow")
203      robotStatusframe.grid(column=0, row =3, sticky=(N,E))
204      Label(robotStatusframe, text= "MTR DIR" ).grid( row=0,column=0,sticky=(N,E))
205      Label(robotStatusframe, text= "MTR SPEED").grid(row=1,column=0,sticky=(N,E))
206      Label(robotStatusframe, text= "MSG Sys").grid(row=3,sticky=(N,E))
207      bFrame = LabelFrame(root,width=100, height=15)
208      bFrame.grid(column=0,columnspan=4, row=10, sticky=(N,W,S))
209      Button(bFrame, text = "WAV PLAY", fg="green",
210      command = wavPlayer).grid(column=1, row=0)
211      Button(bFrame, text = "Text Speak", fg="yellow",
212      command = txtPlayer).grid(column=2, row=0)
213      Button(bFrame, text = "Camera", fg="blue",
214      command = cameraSetup).grid(column=3, row=0)
215      Button(bFrame, text = "SHUTDOWN", fg="red",
216      command = callEXIT).grid(column=7, row=0)
217  def displayUPDATING():
218      while True:
219          updatedisplay.msgFromMax()        # refresh the display
220          time.sleep(.5)
```

Illustration 41

```
221  def myTimer():
222      while True:
223          MOTOR.MTR.myFailSafe= MOTOR.MTR.myFailSafe + 1
224          if MOTOR.MTR.myFailSafe > 500000:          #approx 3 -5 seconds
225              MOTOR.MTR.myFailSafe=0                  #reset counter
226              MOTOR.stopAll()
227              MOTOR.MTR.sysMsg='AUTO STOP '           # display on message pannel
228  def threadstart():
229      dispTh=Thread(target=displayUPDATING, name='dispMSG',args=())
230      timeTh=Thread(target=myTimer, name='myStopTimer',args=())
231      dispTh.setDaemon(True)        #must set all child threads before starting
232      timeTh.setDaemon(True)
233      try:
234          print ('starting dispTh')
235          dispTh.start()
236          print ('starting timeTh')
237          timeTh.start()
238      except:
239          print ('ERROR starting thread')
240  if __name__=='__main__':
241      root = Tk()
242      root.title( "Max2 Control Center" )
243      root.geometry( "500x400+40+30" ) #width, height, placement on x and  y axis
244      setupCanvas()
245      menubar = Menu(root)          #pull down menu section
246      root.config(menu=menubar)
247      filemenu = Menu(menubar, tearoff=0)
248      filemenu.add_separator()
249      filemenu.add_command(label="Exit", command=callEXIT)
250      menubar.add_cascade(menu=filemenu, label='File')
251      MOTOR.Motor.controlPins(MOTOR.MTR)          #define GPIO pins
252      moveHeadFINAL.setupTk(0)
253      updatedisplay=UpdateDisplay(root)        #get the initial display filled in
254      displayStaticStuff()
255      threadstart()
256      mainloop()# Thank you, best of luck, see website for additional materials
```

Illustration 42

GPIO setup Motor Control

This module is imported by our master control program. I expect this program to always be imported so I have not set it up to run independently. Our first task is to define a class Motor. Using class adds structure to your program and makes it a lot, a very lot, easier to share variables between functions and programs. I have attempted to make the names descriptive as to their purpose. The Raspberry Pi GPIO is a 'little touchy' and I believe the functions are evolving. While at the time I am writing this I am using the latest release, I expect there will be changes. One very simple one is that at this point you need to operate the Python program as 'root' to have access to GPIO. I found that to setup the GPIO pins for PWM I had to set them as output first. Fine, just turn power off while setting up, at least for how this program works.

The functions for Motor control are called from our master control program. The way I am using the H-Bridge I am not enabling H-Bridge pins 1 or 9. I have set the PWM frequency at 50 for my drive motors, you may need to adjust that for your motors. Before I start a Motor I make sure it is powered off for the opposite direction. (If both forward and backward on motor will not turn, you may damage the H-Bridge.)

The bumper presented some interesting challenges. I am using GPIO 11. As you can see in the code the GPIO is setup as input, with a pull up and we added most importantly a callback command to be executed when GPIO.RISING. I played with this a lot and there are no doubt better ways to do it but at least it works. If you have tried any of the many practice programs that are out on the web I am sure you ran in to what is called 'bounce'. In simple terms, if you press a button multiple signals may be sent. In this case not too worried about multiple signals as we are just stopping the motors and displaying a message. I did include the 'bouncetime' option as it is a simple step. What is a concern are false signals. I am not sure exactly where they are coming from; my guess is that enough of a charge builds up in the wire that a signal is generated. I noticed this when running the motors at a low speed. You may need to add a resistor in the bumper line. I am running without the resistor and have not included one in the diagram as the errors were very infrequent.

In this module I update the MTR variables quite frequently. When our thread for update of display executes the messages are displayed on our master control display.

```
      max2Module3FINAL.py - /home/pi/MAX3 - Geany                          _ □ x

      File  Edit  Search  View  Document  Project  Build  Tools  Help

      max2Module3FINAL.py  X

      1     # Max2Module3FINAL.py  Support for max2ControlFINAL.py
      2     # using Python 3.2.3   setup to run on Linux
      3     #author Herb  11/14/2013
      4     # company name RyMax, Inc. www.rymax.biz
      5     # for personal hobby use only, include references to RyMax Inc. for
      6     # resale or commercial use contact RyMax, Inc. for written persmission.
      7     import RPi.GPIO as GPIO
      8     GPIO.setmode(GPIO.BOARD)
      9     from time import sleep
      10    import time
      11
      12    class Motor:
      13        def __init__(Data,sysMsg,RightDC,LeftDC,RightMtrDir,LeftMtrDir,
      14            displayRightDC,displayLeftDC,p15,p18,p16,p22,p11,myFailSafe):
      15            Data.sysMsg=sysMsg
      16            Data.RightDC=RightDC              #Duty Cycle or Power Right motor
      17            Data.LeftDC=LeftDC                #Duty Cycle or Power Left motor
      18            Data.RightMtrDir=RightMtrDir
      19            Data.LeftMtrDir=LeftMtrDir
      20            Data.displayRightDC=displayRightDC
      21            Data.displayLeftDC=displayLeftDC
      22            Data.p15=p15                     #Left Motor Reverse (proto plate 22)
      23            Data.p18=p18                     #Right Motor Reverse (proto plate 24)
      24            Data.p16=p16                     #Left Motor Forward (proto plate 23)
      25            Data.p22=p22                     #Right Motor Forward (proto plate 25)
      26            Data.p11=p11                     #Front Bumper (proto plate 17)
      27            Data.myFailSafe=myFailSafe           #Counter for FailSafe stop

      line: 96 / 96   col: 0   sel: 0   INS   TAB   mode: Win (CRLF)   encoding: UTF-8   filetype: Python   scope: stopAll
```

Illustration 43

File   Edit   Search   View   Document   Project   Build   Tools   Help

max2Module3FINAL.py

```python
    def controlPins(Data):
        print ('at setup controlPins')
        GPIO.setup(15, GPIO.OUT)
        Data.p15=""
        Data.p15=GPIO.PWM(15, 50)      #frequency at 50 this worked best
        Data.p15.stop()
        GPIO.setup(22, GPIO.OUT)
        Data.p22=""
        Data.p22=GPIO.PWM(22, 50)
        Data.p22.stop()
        GPIO.setup(16, GPIO.OUT)
        Data.p16=""
        Data.p16=GPIO.PWM(16, 50)
        Data.p16.stop()
        GPIO.setup(18, GPIO.OUT)
        Data.p18=""
        Data.p18=GPIO.PWM(18, 50)
        Data.p18.stop()
        GPIO.setup(11, GPIO.IN,pull_up_down=GPIO.PUD_UP)
        GPIO.add_event_detect(11, GPIO.RISING,callback=bumperPush,bouncetime=300)
        Data.myFailSafe=0
MTR = Motor('Ready',100,100,'Stop','Stop',0,0,'','','','','',0)

def bumperPush(channel):
    print ('Bumper contact')
    MTR.sysMsg="BUMPER HIT"
    stopAll()
    time.sleep(5)
```

line: 96 / 96   col: 0   sel: 0   INS   TAB   mode: Win (CRLF)   encoding: UTF-8   filetype: Python   scope: stopAll

Illustration 44

```
56  def rev():
57      print ('at REVERSE')
58      MTR.p16.stop()
59      MTR.p22.stop()
60      MTR.p15.start(0)
61      MTR.p18.start(0)
62      MTR.p15.ChangeDutyCycle(0)
63      MTR.p18.ChangeDutyCycle(0)
64      MTR.sysMsg="Reverse"
65      try:
66          MTR.p18.ChangeDutyCycle(MTR.RightDC)
67          MTR.p15.ChangeDutyCycle(MTR.LeftDC)
68      except:
69          print ('Error on Fwd ChangeDutyCycle')
70          pass
71  def fwd():
72      print ('at FORWARD')
73      MTR.p15.stop()
74      MTR.p18.stop()
75      MTR.p16.start(100)
76      MTR.p22.start(100)
77      MTR.sysMsg="Forward"
78      try:
79          MTR.p22.ChangeDutyCycle(MTR.RightDC)
80          MTR.p16.ChangeDutyCycle(MTR.LeftDC)
81      except:
82          print ('Error on Fwd ChangeDutyCycle')
83          pass
84  def stopAll():
85      MTR.p15.stop()
86      MTR.p18.stop()
87      MTR.p16.stop()
88      MTR.p22.stop()
89      MTR.sysMsg="STOP ALL"
90      MTR.LeftMtrDir = "STOP"
91      MTR.RightMtrDir = "STOP"
92      MTR.RightDC=0
93      MTR.LeftDC=0
94      MTR.displayRightDC=MTR.RightDC
95      MTR.displayLeftDC=MTR.LeftDC
96
```

line: 96 / 96   col: 0   sel: 0   INS   TAB   mode: Win (CRLF)   encoding: UTF-8   filetype: Python   scope: stopAll

Illustration 45

Now that you have all the modules working, time to run. Select your control program 'maxControlFinal.py' from Geany and select 'Execute'. Or if you are running from a command prompt enter

 "python3 maxControlFinal.py".

The 'Max2 Control Center' window should be displayed along with the Max Move Head window. If you click on the 'WAV PLAY' 'Text Speak' and 'Camera' buttons you should see all the windows opened and ready to go.

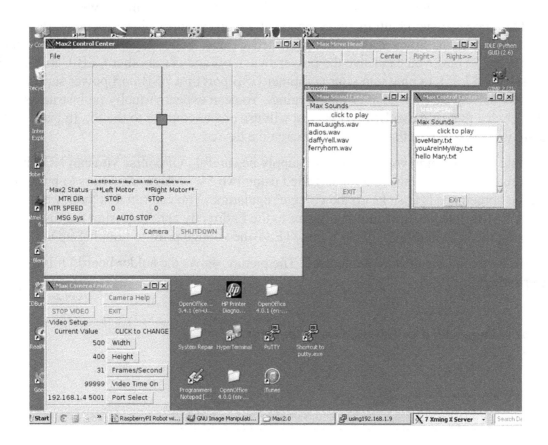

Illustration 46

RASPBERRY Pi POWER

Our Pi needs 5volts, with the WiFi and camera running a fair amount of current is required. Unless you have a long extension cord you will want to run the Pi from a battery. At first I thought I could run it from a 9.6 V 600mAh battery. Like what the remote controlled cars run on. I was not happy with this, seemed to work for a short period, but I think the drain was too much on the battery to continue, or maybe just a bad battery. To get around this I went to a Power Sonic, Model PS-1212, 12 Volt 1.4 Amp. Hr battery. Once again it did not run too long. I tried measuring how many milliamps were needed to run the Pi. My guess is that a bare-bones Pi with just the SD card needs about 170-200 milliamps. When you add in the WiFi I am guessing about another 200 milliamps, then you add the piCamera. While I did try using my multimeter I was unsuccessful in getting reading as items on the Pi powered up. Seemed like the multimeter went out of range and the Pi just stopped. The standard wall power supply says 5V and 1A. The Pi runs just fine from the standard wall power supply. So just trying to bench mark what we need I guess we need a maximum of 1A at 5V to a minimum of 600 milliamps. I played with several batteries, even adding several capacitors; the results were not satisfactory with a single battery. I built a battery pack using three 9.6V 600mAh – 750mAh. This is working nicely. Not sure how long MAX can run, but looks like more than an hour.

While getting this homemade battery pack is working I ordered from Adafruit the USB Battery Pack for Raspberry Pi – 10000mAh, price $49.95, ID:1566. While there are other choices I went with this. Happy to see the device has a power switch built in. Nice options with this device. First, you plug into the standard Pi power input, so you are going in via a somewhat protected service. Second, you do not need to build the voltage regular board. Third, you can leave the power switch off and use another USB-Cable -A/MicroB cord(adafruit ID 592 $3.95) to plug into your computer USB port or a USB port power supply 5V 1A (adafruit PID: 501 $5.95)wall plug adapter for charging. You can expect virtually no instructions with the device. On the device there are two USB ports, you will use one to connect to the Pi. In between the two USB ports there is a MicroB port that you use to charge the device.

If you go the route of developing your own power supply be careful. Of course you can NOT hook this up to your Pi without reducing the voltage to 5volts. I tried using two 5V voltage regulators to bring the 9.6v down to 5v. I put some homemade heat sinks on the voltage regulators. You can run this 5v power into the 5v pin on the Pi. BE AWARE, that you are inputting power to the Pi directly and bypassing the fuse protection that is used when using the built in power supply point. TEST the voltage prior to hooking up to the Pi.

 The diagram shows a mini breadboard being used. The picture shows the solder board. It is a very good idea to add a power switch.

Test the output voltage with a voltmeter, very important.

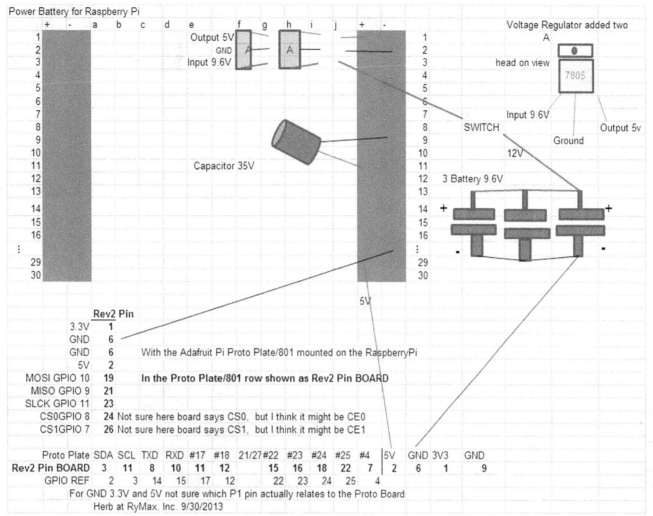

Illustration 47

	Rev2 Pin	
3.3V	1	
GND	6	
GND	6	With the Adafruit Pi Proto Plate/801 mounted on the RaspberryPi
5V	2	
MOSI GPIO 10	19	**In the Proto Plate/801 row shown as Rev2 Pin BOARD**
MISO GPIO 9	21	
SLCK GPIO 11	23	
CS0GPIO 8	24	Not sure here board says CS0, but I think it might be CE0
CS1GPIO 7	26	Not sure here board says CS1, but I think it might be CE1

Proto Plate	SDA	SCL	TXD	RXD	#17	#18	21/27	#22	#23	#24	#25	#4	5V	GND	3V3	GND
Rev2 Pin BOARD	3	11	8	10	11	12		15	16	18	22	7	2	6	1	9
GPIO REF	2	3	14	15	17	12		22	23	24	25	4				

For GND 3.3V and 5V not sure which P1 pin actually relates to the Proto Board

Herb at RyMax, Inc. 9/30/2013

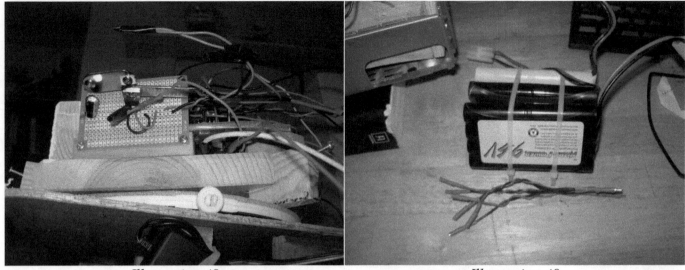

Illustration 48   *Illustration 49*

You may notice the homemade connectors in Illustration 49.

Illustration 50

Illustration 51

MAX2 Motor Battery

For the motors I am using a separate battery. The wiring was shown in the section dealing with the H-Bridge. I recommend that you include a power switch for this battery as well as for the Pi battery.

THE END OR THE BEGINNING

I hope that you have learned a lot and had some fun.

Visit the web site www.rymax.biz for additional information. I would like to learn from your experience, you can e-mail me at herb@rymax.biz.

APPENDIX

Summary for Raspberry Pi Setup

There is a good chance that the steps taken to setup your Raspberry Pi will evolve over time. The following is just a guide as to the steps that I took. While I did build a new OS for this book, you need to expect things to change, and of course I may have forgotten something, but I don't think so. Check out the web for the latest instructions.

Raspberry pi building the SD card		
	I have settled on the debian-wheezy with the desktop that is standard with it LXDE	
	I have used the pc as the source and a desktop running debian-wheezy -linux.	
	download the file from	
see	http://www.raspberrypi.org/downloads	
see	http://elinux.org/RPi_Easy_SD_Card_Setup	
	same for either pc on linux	
	under file manager double click on the file to unzip 2012-12-16-wheezy-raspbian.zip	
Download image 2013-09-25-wheezy-raspian.zip file 577 Mb Version wheezy Kernel 3.6 FILE size 605,227,145 on MY PC Disk		
	this then is used to generate the image file which is approx 2,892,800 KB	
	from Prompt run sha1sum on the img file 2013-09-25-wheezy-raspian.img PRIOR TO UNZIPPING	
	should get following Raspberry Pi download page 99e6b5e6b8cfbf66e34437a74022fcf9744ccb1d	
	takes a few minuets to run MAKE SURE YOU RUN ON THE ZIP FILE	
	I got 99e6b5e6b8cfbf66e34437a74022fcf9744ccb1d 2013-09-25-wheezy-raspbian.img	
Download SD Formatter 4.0 sor SD/SDHC/SDXC		
	https://www.sdcard.org/downloads/formatter_4/	
	I installed My Documents\SDFormatter It put Icon on Desktop	
Make sure you set FORMAT SIZE ADJUSTMENT to ON in the Options menu		
	http://elinux.org/RPi_Hardware_Basic_Setup	
Disk Image Win32		
	down load from	
	http://sourceforge.net/projects/win32diskimager/	
Insert SD in Raspberry Pi and power up the Raspberry Pi		
	should boot to raspi-config	
	select EXPAND-ROOTFS -Expand Root Partion to Fill SD Card I did not want a separate partition	
	then let it reboot should now be able to see full size	
	login pi	
	pwd raspberry	
	sudo raspi-config	
	change password for pi	
	sudo passwd pi	
	enter new password twice	
	enable SSH under advanced options	
	exit raspi-config	
	sudo apt-get update	
	sudo apt-get upgrade	
	suggest a reboot	
	login pi	
	if you want to start the desktop GUI type startx	

Illustration 52

Add user root

To create a root user complete the following, reference to http://www.raspbmc.com/wiki/user/root-access/

You are probably logged in as pi.

sudo passwd root

   system will prompt you for "Enter new UNIX password" and then prompt you to renter it. You should get message "password updated successfully"

Simple DOS commands

Before we go any further, a few quick words on DOS commands. They can do damage, they are not very user friendly; they will destroy without asking twice. So make sure the command you enter is the command that you want and that you know what the command is going to do.

Simple DOS commands, execute from the DOS command prompt. Remember DOS is not case sensitive.
- Dir or dir   – This will give you the contents of the current directory
- Help   – all the commands that are available
- Help dir   – gives you all the options available with dir
- cd {dir name}– change directory, you would add the directory name
- cd ../   – moves up the directory tree one level
- cls   –clear the DOS window screen

logging on to Pi from Windows

Make sure you have started the Xming server. You need to start PuTTY and use the setting shown for PuTTY. You will log-in as 'root'. See the Appendix sections for setting up PuTTY and Xming.

logging on to Pi from Debian-Linux

There are a lot of ways to do this, the following is the simplest method I have found to enable a GUI interface, have a video feed and log-in as the user root. You must have ssh enabled on the Pi. You probably have already set this. You can check by entering on the Pi the following command sudo raspi-config and looking at the Advance Options, A4 and making sure that SSH is enabled.

From a terminal prompt on your Debian-Linux PC enter the command "ssh -X 192.168.1.9 -l root". As I mentioned earlier make sure you use a capital X and a small letter L. You will be asked for the root password. As you can see from the Illustration, I changed to our program directory and started Geany.

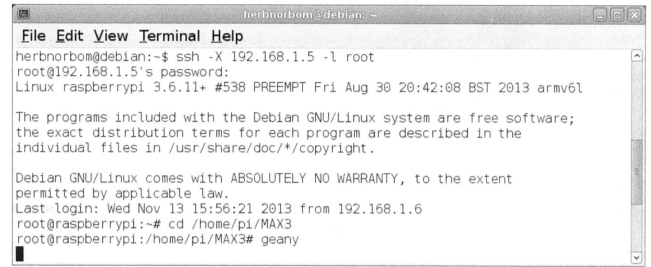

Illustration 53

Starting Netcat and MPlayer Windows

We are only using DOS to start our Netcat program. I am going to create a bat script in the location where my '*cmd*' prompt opened. Adjust the following as needed for your system.

Use a simple text editor, Geany or the DOS edit program to create a simple bat file for starting the video capture. At this point I have downloaded and installed Netcat and MPlayer. In my case both were installed in directories under "My Documents" adjust the bat file or script as needed. But what the script or bat file does is change to the directory where I installed Netcat and issue a list directory command. I then put a second bat file in that directory to actually start Netcat and display the video. While you can combine the two bat files if you like, I kept them separate because I kept playing with the options on the second one and was tired of changing directories. My first bat file is named "raspberryFeed.bat" and it is saved in the directory where the command or DOS prompt opens. It only has two lines, so if you are good at remembering where things are you may not need this bat file. The two lines are:
cd My Documents\Netcat
dir

The second bat file is really the more important one as I will not remember the command to start Netcat. This bat file is named startNETCAT.bat and I saved it in the Netcat directory. I just have one line, you can adjust for example fps, but seems to work best if it matches what you set the camera program at. You can also play with the cache size. For Windows this is the command that I use:
nc.exe -L -p 5001 | ..\mplayer-svn-36442\mplayer.exe -fps 31 -cache 2048 -

nc.exe   is the Netcat program
-L   is for Windows only, instructs program Listen harder, or a persistent listener, like NSA
-p 5001 is the local port that I want to listen to
| the vertical line is the pipe command, what Netcat hears we pipe to mplayer.exe
..\mplayer-svn-36442   is the directory that I installed mplayer.exe in
mplayer.exe   is the program that displays the video that Netcat hears
-fps   frames per second

-cache   size (you can play with and try various sizes)
  – need this last dash to make it work

To end the program use "Ctrl c".

To test you can run the script on the Windows PC. On the Pi you need to start the camera with the command "raspivid -t 9999 -o - | nc 192.168.1.4 5001". Note the IP address is the IP for the Windows PC. A good reference site is: http://www.raspberrypi.org/camera .

starting Netcat and MPlayer Debian-Linux

The start-up is very similar to the Windows version. From a terminal prompt on the Debian-Linux PC I entered the following command which I have saved in a script file. Remember to make your script file executable. That is a small letter L after nc.

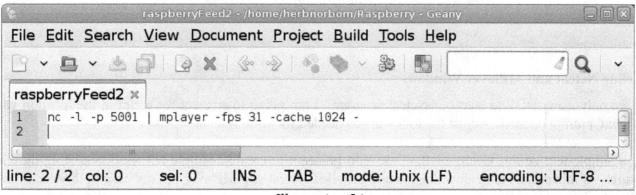

Illustration 54

To test you can run the script in Illustration54 on the Debian-Linux PC. On the Pi you need to start the camera with the command "raspivid -t 9999 -o - | nc 192.168.1.6 5001". Note the IP address is the IP for the Debian-Linux PC. A good reference site is: http://www.raspberrypi.org/camera .
Illustration 55 shows a sample of what the output on the Debian-Linux PC looks like.

Illustration 55

PuTTY for Windows

For our communications you will need PuTTY© installed on your PC. The following describes how to obtain the PuTTY executable. Go to the main PuTTY Download Page. http://www.chiark.greenend.org.uk/~sgtatham/putty/download.html. From this page you can select the appropriate file. I suggest you get the Windows installer for everything except PuTTYtel. At this point the latest release is version .63.

Open PuTTY and click on SSH, make appropriate changes.   For Host Name or IP address I am using the IP address (for the Pi) and Port 22. Under Category select (Connection SSH X11) and Enable X11 forwarding. Under Category Session you can name your file under Saved Sessions, which is a real good idea. There are lots of options you set set, but we are just using PuTTY to setup our Xming communication so our Python program has a GUI interface.

The PuTTY help files should have been included if things are not working.

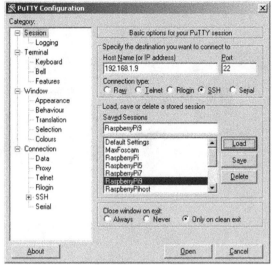

Illustration 56

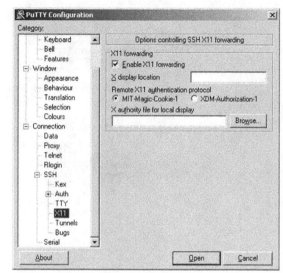

Illustration 57

PuTTY for Debian-Linux

The install is very straight forward. Just run "sudo apt-get install putty". The PuTTY settings are the same as for the Windows version mentioned above. Nice to have but not needed as we will use the standard ssh included with Debian-Linux.

Xming X Server for Windows

This program is needed on your Windows PC to support the GUI interface for our Python Tkinter items. You can download the software from http://sourceforge.net/projects/xming/ . I tried many options, but I think most of my problem in getting it to work was in my not setting up PuTTY. You will need PuTTY for this to work. After you have downloaded Xming you need to run the XLaunch program. I selected "Multiple windows" and on the next screen I selected "Start no client". On the next screen I have checked the "Clipboard" to Start the integrated clipboard manager. On the next screen I saved the configuration and clicked Finish. Th Xming server needs to be running on your PC for our Python tkinter to work.

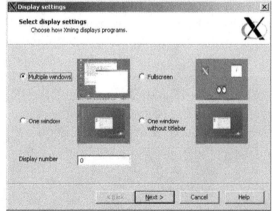

Illustration 58

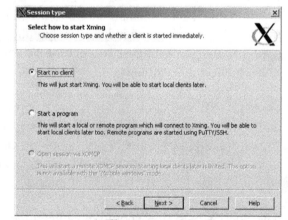

Illustration 59

Geany for Windows

The program has many useful features as well as being a very nice text editor. Go to www.geany.org . The geany-1.2.3.1 setup.exe Full Installer, is approximately 8Mb.

Geany for Raspberry Pi

Pretty straight forward "sudo apt-get install geany". If you want to install on the Debian-Linux PC the same command works.

Netcat for Raspberry Pi and Debian-Linux

This is a very neat program but expect to get warning as to security. You should evaluate your system and determine if risk justifies reward. In my case I went for it. You need to install this software on the Raspberry Pi and on your PC.

On Raspberry Pi and your Debian-Linux PC use the following command.

sudo apt-get install netcat

The program is also available from http://sourceforge.net/projects/nc110/

Netcat For Windows

On Windows try http://nmap.org/download.html#windows there are download instructions and a self installer. This will get you the binaries, if you want the source it is also available. I installed the Netcat software in the "My Documents" directory. You can expect some security warnings, you need to evaluate. While there are other ways to skin the cat I could at least make this work pretty well.

eSpeak for Raspberry Pi

I installed the general eSpeak and not the python-espeak. To install use "sudo apt-get install espeak".

MPlayer Windows

Installation on Windows PC, you can download from http://sourceforge.net/projects/mplayer-win32/ . I installed the software in the "My Documents" directory. Adjust as you desire but you will need to also adjust the bat or script file for starting.

MPlayer for Debian-Linux

For Debian-Linux use "sudo apt-get install mplayer".

H-Bridge

Now that we have the logic down we need to refine our hardware for the motor control. The simplest way I found to do this was with a chip called the H-bridge. There are a number of different H-bridges on the market. There are differences; make sure you get the Data Sheet. For testing if you have some small motors from toys or hand held fans they will work well. As for the auxiliary power supply I show it as 12V, but that will vary for you depending on your motor choice. If you are using some small motors reduce the auxiliary voltage. A 9 volt battery, a voltage regulator or a voltage divider can be used. Many DC motors will run on various voltages, just at different speeds. Don't run too long if not sure, watch for signs of overheating. If you detect the ozone smell shut down the power quickly. It is very easy to burn up a chip at this point. If the

Pi crashes or reboots when you start the motor, check your wiring first. If everything is correct you may need to add some capacitors. Remember when a motor starts up it can draw a strong current. Capacitors hold a charge, so even after you shut off the external power there is power in your circuit. Ground yourself and the board. If you don't have motors you can improvise with the LED's, but you will need more because LED's are not bidirectional for current flow. In place of the H-Bridge you could use a series of mosfet's. I found the low cost H-Bridge much simpler to use. Make sure you select an H-Bridge that has internal clamp diodes to prevent inductive flyback effect from the motors. When a motor suddenly stops a voltage in the opposite direction can occur, you need to prevent this, hence the clamp diodes.

Sound on the Raspberry Pi

To get the sound working make sure you have the latest software. Run 'sudo apt-get update' and 'sudo apt-get upgrade'. I also ran 'sudo apt-get install alsa-utils'. Test run type 'alsamixer' should get a display for volume and various other items. The key for me was in running the command "sudo amixer cset numid=3 1". There is a space between the 3 and the 1.

Building the Robot

Are you ready to build your robot? You can spend as much money as you want, but I tend to be well shall we say thrifty. Let me talk a little about Max. Max is a simple prototype designed to prove concepts, not to look pretty. Max's frame is a salvaged metal case from a cable or satellite control box. The two drive motors are 24 VDC with wheels and built in gearboxes. I purchased them for about $9.00 each. You will want drive motors with gearboxes. I had connectors around so I used those, as I wanted to be able to take Max apart easily. The front wheel is a swivel caster wheel that I had lying around. The head is driven by a small servo motor. The head itself is lid to a trash can with a plastic swivel base from a microwave on a small piece of wood. The bumper is a wood strip on screws with springs and a contact wire. The contact wire is striped ordinary household gauge 10 to 12. You are ready, Go ahead and assemble your robot. As you can see in the pictures there are a lot of wires. I hope as you look at this you can visualize your board. When you get to the point of soldering a board I suggest that you put the H-Bridge in a suitable holder that allows you to remove and replace the chip.

The batteries ride in the metal case. Three 9.6 volt batteries power the Pi and head servo, a voltage regular is required to get the correct 5 volts for the Raspberry Pi. A separate 12 volt battery is for the drive motors. While the drive motors can take up to 24 volts, I decided to stick with the 12 volt battery. For your robot you will need to evaluate the hardware specifications, and consider your future needs. The head is driven by a parallax standard servo. Whichever servo you choose make sure you get the data sheet. There are excellent tutorials on the web about servo's or stepper motors. I am asking you to do your homework and not just rely on the setting I show in the program for running the servo.

Cost and Possible Parts List for the Robot Hardware

PART DESCRIPTION	QTY	Est. Total COST $	NOTES
Metal Chassis Frame	1	0.00	salvaged
Drive Motors with gear box & wheels	2	18.00	All Electronics DCM-351
Stepper Motor Parallax Standard Servo (#900-00005)	1	15.00	
Front Caster	1	0.00	salvaged

PART DESCRIPTION	QTY	Est. Total COST $	NOTES
scrap wood		0.00	salvaged
Various Connectors		2.00	salvaged
Battery pack 9.6 Volt	3	44.97	check out various sources
Battery 12 Volt Rechargeable	1	15.00	for the Raspberry Pi and Servo and drive motors

Debian-Linux Shell Scripts

A few hints for making your scripts executable. Not your Python scripts, Python handles that. You can write your script using any text editor, vi or vim, etc. I

- The file name doesn't need an extension.

- Comments are a line starting with a pound sign '#'

- You need to have permission to execute or run the script. After you have saved your script open a terminal window and go to the directory where you saved the script. Type 'ls -l filename' for example. (small letter 'L') The permissions will be shown. Something like the following table, third row.

position 1	2	3	4	5	6	7	8	9	10
directory flag	User read	User write	User execute	Group read	Group write	Group execute	Other read	Other write	Other execute
-	r	w	-	r	-	-	r	-	-
-	r	w	x	r	-	-	r	-	-

You need to make the script an executable. You can do this from a terminal window be in the directory with your script and type chmod u+x filename. Then retype the ls -l filename and you should see the change as shown on row 4 of the preceding table. (that is a small letter L) To run the script from the terminal window, be in the same directory and type. ./filename or type . filename (Notice the . and space)

Debian-Linux Commands

Before using understand that many of the commands have options that are not shown here. For those who may have forgotten some simple Linux commands, a very quick refresher course follows. This is only the tip of the iceberg, just listing a few. Before we go any further, a few quick words on commands. They can do damage, they are not very user friendly; they will destroy without asking twice. So make sure the command you enter is the command that you want and that you know what the command is going to do. Remember when you execute a command that involves a filename you may want to proceed the filename with a "./". Example "cat ./filename".

cat filname	list contents of file
cat filename > filename2	copy filename to filename2
cat /etc/debian_version	this will show what version of Debian you are running

cat /etc/os-release	will show misc. os information
cd	change to home directory
cd /	change to root directory
cd ..	move up one level in the directory tree
chown newower filename	change the owner of filename to the new owner name
chmod u+x filename	example of changing permission of stk500work for the user to execute
clear	clear the screen can also use Ctrl L
cp filename filename2	copy filename to filname2
date	show current day, date and time
df -h	File systems mounted, size, used, avail Use%, where mounted
dmesg	This will show the devices attached, very useful for finding PL2303 and other serial devices attached
echo $SHELL	to see what shell you are running
find -name filename	find the specified filename
free -m	display memory used and free
id	what user you are and what groups you are in
ifconfig	display connections information, (eth0, lo, wlan0, etc)
ip addr show	show connection addresses
kill number	If you need to stop a runaway process, number is the process ID (PID)
lp filename	print filename to default printer
lpstat -t	show default printer
lsusb	list usb devices running on computer
lsusb -v	run as sudo for a complete list, with v is a verbose list
mkdir filename	make a new directory
more filename	list the file, will do in pages
mv filename filname2	move or rename filename to filname2
pwd	to see what your current directory is
whoami	to see what user you are
ps -p$	generates a process error but shows options
ps -T or ps	show all processes on this terminal
ps -A	show all processes running on computer
ps aux	show all process running on computer, user, PID & more
pstree	show all processes in a tree format
ps -p$$	show current PID TTY TIME CMD
uname -a	display version and kernel

rm filename	delete file specified
reboot	do an immediate shutdown and then reboot
reset	use when console has character map a mess, resets to standard
rmdir directory	remove specified directory
rm -r directory	remove specified directory and contents of the directory
shutdown -h now	shutdown the computer now, you may need sudo in front of command
who	list all users

Reference Sites
The following sites have useful information.

Raspberry

http://www.raspberrypi.org

http://www.element14.com/community/groups/roadtest?ICID=roadtest_subnav

http://www.engadget.com/2012/09/05/cambridge-university-raspberry-pi-guide/

http://www.engadget.com/2012/09/04/raspberry-pi-getting-started-guide-how-to/

http://www.raspberrypi.org/downloads

http://elinux.org/RPiconfig

http://elinux.org/RPi_VerifiedPeripherals

http://elinux.org/RPi_Distributions

http://elinux.org/R-Pi_Troubleshooting

http://elinux.org/RPi_Hardware#Power

http://shallowsky.com/blog/hardware/pi-battery.html

http://elinux.org/RPi_raspi-config

http://asliceofraspberrypi.blogspot.com/2013/05/displaying-system-information-and.html

Raspberry - Camera

http://elinux.org/Rpi_Camera_Module

Raspberry – Sound

http://elinux.org/R-Pi_Troubleshooting#Sound

Raspberry – GPIO

http://elinux.org/RPi_Tutorial_Easy_GPIO_Hardware_%26_Software

http://learn.adafruit.com/adafruits-raspberry-pi-lesson-4-gpio-setup/configuring-gpio

https://npmjs.org/package/pi-gpio

https://code.google.com/p/raspberry-gpio-python/wiki/BasicUsage

http://www.cl.cam.ac.uk/projects/raspberrypi/tutorials/robot/cheat_sheet/

http://www.thirdeyevis.com/pi-page-2.php

http://raspi.tv/2013/rpi-gpio-basics-5-setting-up-and-using-outputs-with-rpi-gpio

Xming

http://sourceforge.net/projects/xming/

http://www.straightrunning.com/XmingNotes/pixming.php

eSpeak

http://espeak.sourceforge.net/commands.html

http://www.thegeekstuff.com/2010/03/espeak-speech-synthesizer-for-ubuntu/

Python

www.sourceforge.net
www.docs.python.org
www.astro.ufl.edu
www.sthurlow.com
www.learnpython.org
http://www.astro.ufl.edu/~warner/prog/python.html
www.tutorialspoint.com/python/index.htm
https://developers.google.com/edu/python
http://anh.cs.luc.edu/python/hands-on/handsonHtml/handson.html
http://www.python.org/dev/peps/pep-0008/
http://docs.python.org/2/library/subprocess.html
http://docs.python.org/2/tutorial/errors.html
http://docs.python.org/2/library/stdtypes.html
http://zetcode.com/lang/python/datatypes/
http://www.ibm.com/developerworks/library/os-python1/
http://pguides.net/python-tutorial/python-string-methods/
http://mkaz.com/solog/python-string-format
http://infohost.nmt.edu/tcc/help/pubs/python/web/old-str-format.html
http://www.tutorialspoint.com/python/python_strings.htm
http://docs.python.org/2/library/string.html
http://docs.python.org/2/library/queue.html
http://www.blog.pythonlibrary.org/2012/08/01/python-concurrency-an-example-of-a-queue/
http://stackoverflow.com/questions/2846653/python-multithreading-for-dummies
http://www.tutorialspoint.com/python/python_multithreading.htm
http://docs.python.org/2/library/time.html

Tkinter

http://effbot.org/tkinterbook/grid.htm
http://infohost.nmt.edu/tcc/help/pubs/tkinter/web/index.html
http://www.tkdocs.com/tutorial/windows.html
http://pages.cpsc.ucalgary.ca/~saul/personal/archives/Tcl-Tk_stuff/tcl_examples/
http://effbot.org/tkinterbook/

http://www.pythonware.com/library/tkinter/introduction/hello-tkinter.htm
http://www.tutorialspoint.com/python/python_gui_programming.htm
http://www.beedub.com/book/2nd/TKINTRO.doc.html
 http://zetcode.com/gui/tkinter/menustoolbars/
http://effbot.org/tkinterbook/menu.htm
http://infohost.nmt.edu/tcc/help/pubs/tkinter/web/menu.html
http://www.tutorialspoint.com/python/tk_messagebox.htm
http://effbot.org/tkinterbook/canvas.htm
http://www.tutorialspoint.com/python/tk_canvas.htm

Linux

http://steve-parker.org/sh/intro.shtml

http://linuxtutorial.info/modules.php?name=MContent&pageid=329

http://en.wikibooks.org/wiki/Linux_For_Newbies/Command_Line

Hardware

All Electronics	http://allelectronics.com/
Marlin P. Jones	http://www.mpja.com/
Mouser Electronics	http://www.mouser.com/Home.aspx
DigiKey Electronics	http://www.digikey.com/
MCM Electronics	http://www.mcmelectronics.com/
Adafruit Industries	http://www.adafruit.com/
Sure Electronics	http://www.sureelectronics.net/
Electronix Express	http://www.elexp.com/index.htm
Atbatt.com	http://www.atbatt.com/sitemap.html
Parallax	http://www.parallax.com/product/900-00005

Electrical Knowledge and Circuits

www.circuitlab.com
http://led.linear1.org/1led.wiz

http://www.directron.com/fsbguide.html

http://www.bcae1.com/ohmslaw.htm

http://www.hobby-hour.com/electronics/resistorcalculator.php

http://en.wikipedia.org/wiki/Voltage_divider

http://electronics.stackexchange.com/questions/13746/why-does-a-resistor-need-to-be-on-the-anode-of-an-led

http://www.coilgun.info/theorycapacitors/capacitors2.htm

http://www.atbatt.com/batterytimes/how-to-wire-6v-batteries-in-series-or-parallel-configuration/

Various Pictures of Completed Max2

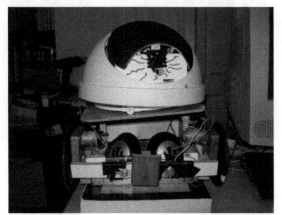

Illustration 60

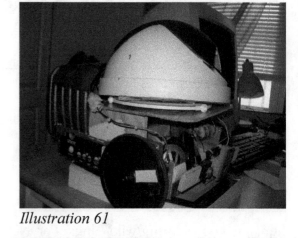

Illustration 61

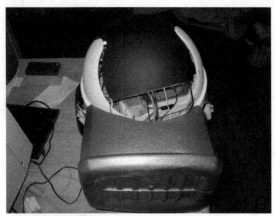

Illustration 62

Illustration 63

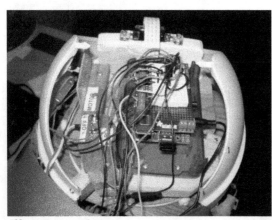

Illustration 64

Illustration 65